THE
UNPARALLELED
Gospel

LUKE

KIE BOWMAN

FOREWORD BY JEREMIAH JOHNSTON, PhD

Auxano
PRESS

ISBN: 978-0-578-10937-4

Published by Auxano Press, Traveler's Rest, South Carolina. www.AuxanoPress.com.

Cover design: Crosslin Creative.net

Page Design and Layout: David Hommel, Church Hill, Tennessee

Printed in the United States of America

18 19 20 21 22 23—6 5 4 3 2 1

I dedicate this work to my dear mother,

Wanda L. Bowman,

who first taught me about Jesus.

I love you, Mom.

Contents

Acknowledgments

I want to thank some key people who have, in unique ways, contributed to the completion of this book.

The congregation of Hyde Park Baptist/The Quarries has a deep commitment to making the gospel of Jesus Christ known in Austin and beyond. I am blessed to have led them as pastor for more than twenty years; they inspire and encourage me. I have the best job in the world!

My church staff has encouraged and supported me throughout this project by helping me carve out the time I needed for research and writing. Becky Shipp, Toni Casteel, and Lois Gamble were instrumental in proofreading. The cover art was developed by Katherine Drye. I am grateful to each one for the capable support.

I am also grateful to Dr. Ken Hemphill and his team at Auxano Press for the opportunity to partner with them as we work together to help people grow in their knowledge of the Word of God.

In addition to these other personal acknowledgments, I am indebted to a host of New Testament scholars who have written about Luke. While I have attempted to give credit where it is necessary, my thinking about Luke has undoubtedly been influenced over the years by many other teachers. So my thoughts expressed as my own in this work have naturally been informed by the thoughts of others.

I am ever grateful for Tina, my wife of thirty-five-plus years. She has been so willing and patient in allowing me the time to complete this work.

Foreword

Can you imagine your story without God? Without faith? How might your life have turned out had you never heard the life-transforming message that God loves you so much He sent His only Son to die in your place? What if you had never heard the name of Jesus? What if there were no churches in your community? What if no crosses or spires or other vestiges of Christianity spotted the skies of your town? What if you had never heard of the Golden Rule or good Samaritan or prodigal son? Well, this reality was exactly what Dr. Luke was faced with in the second half of the first century AD as the shimmering dawn of Christianity began to rise over the Mediterranean world of the Roman Empire. The world needed a new message. The canvas was blank, and little did Luke know he was the one chosen by God to pass on stories that would echo for eternity.

The importance of Luke's contribution to the New Testament and Christian origins can hardly be overstated. Luke includes more parables (the stories Jesus shared) of Jesus than any other Gospel, and those stories continue to resonate and influence culture today: the good Samaritan (Luke 10:30-37), the rich fool (12:16-21), and the prodigal son (15:11-32) are almost universally known by those with or without a faith tradition.

The casual reader of the Bible might be surprised to learn Luke contributes more content to the New Testament than any of the other biblical authors. Not only is the Gospel of Luke the longest canonical Gospel (96 pages in

Nestle-Aland's Greek NT) by page numbers, but it also has more verses (1,151) than the other Gospels (1,071 in Matthew, 678 in Mark, and 869 in John). What's more, Luke's Gospel is the only Gospel with a sequel: the book of Acts. The Holy Spirit led Luke not only to introduce the life and ministry of Jesus, but he also provides a vivid, firsthand account of the church turning the world upside down (see Acts 17:6), energized by the same Spirit that raised Jesus from the dead (Acts 1:8). Papyrus 45 or P45 (AD 250) is an early New Testament manuscript, which is part of the Chester Beatty Papyri collection and contains portions of the Gospel of Luke and book of Acts, a remarkable early witness to the importance of Luke's two-part masterpiece.

Though Luke is never mentioned explicitly as the author of the Gospel that bears his name, there is compelling evidence both internally and externally. Indeed, of all four Gospels, the case for Luke's authorship is most substantial. Irenaeus (AD 130–202), the early church leader, stated Luke was "inseparable" from the apostle Paul (see *Against Heresies* 3.14.1). Justin Martyr (AD 100–165) described Luke as providing a "memoir of Jesus" and also his close companionship with Paul (see *Dialogue with Trypho* 103.19). Tertullian (AD 155–240) characterizes the Gospel of Luke as a digest from Paul himself (see *Against Marcion* 4.2.2; 4.5.3).

Luke's theological emphasis is unparalleled and is as fresh today as it was in the first century. He emphasizes the need to reach the marginalized and outcasts: poor, sick, and even "sinful" Gentiles will be included in the Jesus program of God's kingdom. Luke is also concerned about possessions and the evil of materialism. If one cares about social justice, one will love and appreciate the Gospel of Luke (Luke 3:7-20, "What shall we do? . . . share with him who has none" [vv. 10-11]). Again and again we hear of the compassion of Jesus in Luke. Luke also emphasizes unity. The gospel or "good news" is for all people; none are excluded. Luke knows his Bible too. And by "his Bible," I mean the Hebrew Scriptures (Old Testament). Luke shows how the Old Testament is fulfilled in Christ, both in His resurrection (see ch. 24) and the Great Commission. Luke makes clear that Jesus was "full of the Holy Spirit" (4:1), that the Spirit gave him "power" (4:14), and "joy" (10:21). For Luke, no gift is more valuable than the gift one receives when our heavenly Father gives the Holy Spirit "to those who ask Him" (11:13). Finally, Luke has been described as the Evangelist of Prayer, because again and again Luke emphasizes the intentionality of prayer in the life of Jesus and the early church. Only Luke reveals how Jesus often went off alone to pray (6:12; 9:28). The theological emphases in the Gospel of Luke are illustrated so powerfully in the example of Dr. J. Kie Bowman and his influential preaching, pastoring, and prayer ministry emanating out of Hyde Park Baptist Church in Austin, Texas.

In this fascinating book, Dr. Bowman takes us on a fast-paced, twelve-chapter journey through the Gospel of Luke only using material that is unique to Luke ("L" material not found in any other Gospel). The "L" or Luke-only material comprises 485 verses or 40 percent of Luke's total narrative. Using the latest research, Dr. Bowman provides fresh insights, powerful application, and convicting points that inspire the reader to live an unparalleled, Gospel-centric life. A master communicator and scholar to be sure, Dr. Bowman's gift is not leaving anyone behind in his writing.

The most learned Bible student will find *The Unparalleled Gospel* compelling and loaded with notes and citations; while the first-time or newish Bible reader will enjoy using this powerful resource as a faithful companion illuminating the special place of Luke's Gospel. I am grateful for Dr. Bowman's love for prayer and God's Word. I am also deeply appreciative of Dr. Bowman's desire for people to know the One who loves us with an "everlasting love" (Jer. 31:3). *The Unparalleled Gospel*, to be sure, is a book to be studied as much as it is to be read; but make no mistake, within these pages you will be reminded of the greatness of God's love for you. I am impressed by the skillfulness and depth of this book and know you will be challenged spiritually and stimulated intellectually as you turn the pages.

Jeremiah J. Johnston, PhD
Christian Thinkers Society
Houston, Texas

Introduction

Why are there four Gospels? The question seems simple enough on the surface. After all, wouldn't four different friends have their own unique perspective of a fifth? For the average reader that may be a sufficient answer; and, in a sense, it's an accurate, although incomplete, explanation. However, for the believer or skeptic interested in how and why the New Testament came to us in its current form, the issue goes deeper and deserves thoughtful consideration.

Once we begin digging beneath the surface, the subject gets even more curious. For example, the first three Gospels, called the "Synoptic Gospels" due to their easily identifiable similarities, cover much of the same content; and they are, in fact, identical in places. There are, however, unique and unmistakable differences. For instance, Mark is clearly the shortest Gospel, and most New Testament scholars believe his was the first written Gospel. Matthew includes almost all of Mark, yet it is twice as long. In fact, all of the original material of Mark, not found in the others, constitutes only about two pages of information. Matthew obviously covers much of the same material as Mark but usually in much greater detail and, in addition, contains a considerable amount of new information about Jesus not found in Mark at all.

This unusual feature of striking similarities and differences is true of all the Gospels. In fact, when reviewing the one miracle of Jesus that occurs in all four Gospels, we discover an excellent example of both the agreements and differences found in the four Gospels. In the account of the feeding of five thousand, for instance, 59 percent of the Gospel of Matthew is drawn from the Gospel of Mark. Similarly, Matthew and Luke share about 44 percent of the same material, while Luke only retains 40 percent of Mark. John's Gospel then explodes the matter further. John only retains, or agrees with, Mark 8.5 percent of the time and shares the same amount with Matthew. When comparing John with Luke, only 6.5 percent of the material is the same. In fact, John uses only eight of the same Greek words to tell the same story the others had previously told.[1]

Clearly, John's material is the most unique of the four Gospels and covers details not shared in over 90 percent of the other three. John was an eyewitness who vividly remembered and intentionally included information about Jesus that the others, for their own purposes, chose not to use. Many of those differences have to do with the Synoptics' interest in the Galilean ministry of Jesus, while John is more focused on describing the Judean ministry of Jesus.

If all of this seems like statistical overload, indulge me a moment longer. Since John has a separate agenda with so much unique material, the focus falls back to the question of why the other three are so alike in places while so completely dissimilar in others. Pressing the point even further reveals the interesting fact that the three Synoptic Gospels often share verbatim language, suggesting Matthew and Luke used Mark as a source. Yet, despite clear dependence on Mark, both Matthew and Luke often suddenly diverge in other directions. For example, when Matthew and Luke are in agreement, it is almost always material drawn virtually verbatim from Mark; but when they stray from Mark's narrative, they not only introduce material completely separate from anything found in Mark but also often are completely unique from each other.[2] Why?

We believe the Holy Spirit led the authors to write their Gospels by inspiring them to choose intelligently the material that met their needs as individual communicators and advocates for the gospel. The inspired background of the Gospels, therefore, helps explain their uniqueness, coupled with the fact they were written to different audiences with individual needs and questions.

Since the biblical writers were not limited to a rigid or superimposed structure, we are brought back to consider the questions surrounding the unusual mix of similarities and differences found in the Synoptics. Since Matthew and Luke only occasionally combine to share material not found in Mark, this makes Luke the most unique in the sense that he introduces the most material not found in the other two. That uniqueness in Luke is the rationale behind this current study. Luke is a Gospel without parallel. That's the basis of this book.

Every chapter of this work is a study of a story found nowhere else in the New Testament or a perspective of a more familiar event, such as the birth story or the crucifixion, told from Luke's particular perspective, with additional material separate and unique from the other writers. What is remarkable is this: the entire story of Jesus, from His divine birth, to the cross, the resurrection, and the ascension, can be told from material unique to Luke alone. When the parables of Jesus are added to the mix, Luke looks even more compelling. He relates some of the most familiar and provocative of Jesus's parables found in the New Testament. Luke is unparalleled.

Luke's Gospel presents us with a powerful and personal portrait of the most well-known and closely scrutinized life in history. While Luke admittedly and deliberately shares a similar structure and story arc with the other Synoptics, his story about Jesus is like nothing else.

Who Is Luke?

The Writings Themselves

There are at least three ways to know Luke the man. First, we can read and study his two-volume work, Luke-Acts. From that vantage point we observe patterns emerging. For one thing, he is overtly concerned with God's work through specific events in history. He makes that clear from the introduction of the Gospel. He addresses both volumes to a believer named Theophilus, who may have been a wealthy patron responsible for the financial support of Luke's extensive two-volume writing project.[3] Luke insists he has been aware of "many" other efforts to tell the story of Jesus and clearly respects the value of those efforts since he suggests all of them attempt to tell the story of Jesus and the things "accomplished among us," in keeping with the eyewitness accounts (1:1). The fact he uses the word "many" suggests there were credible written documents about the life of Jesus that we no longer possess but were still commonly available at the time of Luke's writing. Luke intended to add to the available material from the perspective of a historian who had "followed all things closely for some time past" (v. 3).

One of the uniquenesses of Luke's contribution to the literature about Jesus is his concern to place the actions of the Spirit, angels, and miracles directly alongside the activities of paranoid politicians, ruthless kings, and the forgotten, marginalized, and poor Jewish people struggling through their normal lives. In other words, Luke saw no contradiction between the reality of Jesus's miraculous birth and ministry and the gritty reality realized daily by the Roman and Jewish political and religious leaders and the people they ruled.

Luke, more than any of the other Gospel writers, takes extraordinary pains to position the events of his narrative in a historical context using references familiar to his readers. For instance, a twentieth-century New Testament scholar described it succinctly when he observed Luke almost immediately mentions Herod, a figure well known even in secular history. Luke nestles the birth of Jesus "in the broader context of the Roman empire by referring to the decree of Caesar Augustus at whose command Quirinius conducted a census."[4] The same author goes on to compile an impressive list of ways Luke demonstrated his grasp of the geopolitical context into which the Gospel came. For instance, John the Baptist "received the Word of the Lord during the fifteenth year of the reign of Tiberius Caesar while Pontius Pilate was governor of Judea, Herod was Tetrarch of Galilee, his brother, Phillip, was Tetrarch of Iturea and Trachonitis, Lysanias was Tetrarch of Abilene, and Annas and Caiaphas were high priests."[5]

Luke's interest in historical details is expanded even further in the book of Acts to include geographical and political names and titles extending beyond the nation of

Israel and into the Roman Empire, including the Middle East and Europe. These details are significant to us because we are attempting to know and understand the man who wrote more of the New Testament than any other author. What stands out is his unusually comprehensive grasp of the complex politics of the ancient world and his conviction God was actually moving and working in a historical context. The modern critique that religion is an "opiate" or simply a mythological construct to delude superstitious people would be lost completely on a real-world author like Luke. For him, God is not "pie in the sky by and by," as the old saying goes. Instead, in Luke's writings we encounter the God who is working in our world now, to call real people to Himself and establish His kingdom.

One final observation about Luke gleaned from his writings might be helpful at this point. Luke's use of the Greek language is of an extremely high quality and is the most sophisticated in the New Testament (with the possible exception of the book of Hebrews). Clearly, Luke was well educated with an erudite grasp of world events, political complexities, language, and culture. Is it any wonder we can study Luke with a sense of gratitude that a man of his caliber felt God's call to tell the story of Jesus in an orderly and historically reliable manner?

Both Luke and Acts are approximately the same length, the two longest books in the New Testament, and comprise the most material written by one author in the New Testament. From that perspective believers will benefit by spending more time understanding Luke's writings since Luke, in terms of total words, wrote even more of our New Testament than the apostle Paul.

What the Bible Says about Luke

The second way to know Luke the man is from the internal evidence found in passages of Scripture where he is mentioned. Of significant importance in understanding Luke is his close association with the apostle Paul. In some sense it is fair to say Paul discipled Luke, and we should reasonably conclude a heavy Pauline influence in Luke's writings. Paul referred to Luke by name, once calling him "the beloved physician" (Col. 4:14). The word *beloved* is used repeatedly in the New Testament as God's identification of Jesus as His "beloved Son" (Matt. 3:17; Mark 1:11, etc.) and can refer to a chosen or favored person or group (Rom. 11:28; 16:5, etc.). Paul also called Luke a "physician," a word obviously referring to those who practiced the science of healing and medicine in the first century.

No doubt Paul was extremely dependent on the companionship of Luke during some of the most memorable adventures in the early days of the spread of the gospel. Luke's knowledge of medicine, no matter how crude it may have been by modern standards, must have been extremely important to Paul and those earliest missionaries as they crisscrossed the Roman Empire through parts of Asia, the Middle East, and Europe.

Looking even more closely at Paul's mention of Luke, we notice he refers to his coworker not as "a beloved physician" but as "the beloved physician," suggesting Luke had gained notoriety in his own right even before he wrote Luke-Acts. In other words, he was *the* beloved physician not only of Paul but also known and beloved by a much wider audience. It stands to reason Luke had become well known since he was the frequent traveling coworker with the apostle Paul. Luke's notoriety helps us understand how his writings might have been quickly welcomed and accepted by the early church and then more readily and rapidly copied for wider distribution.

Paul also says Luke was with him while the apostle was in prison contemplating his own death (2 Tim. 4:6-7). In a poignant statement, in what would become the last few words written by the apostle, we read, "Luke alone is with me" (2 Tim. 4:11). Anyone who has ever stood by the graveside of a loved one probably identifies with the experience of remembering the last conversations and last words had with the deceased. Last words add a sentimental dimension to our memories. Among Paul's last words we find a clue about the loyal and committed friendship of Luke during a difficult time in the apostle's life. Can you imagine the depth of the conversations held in that prison cell between the two men who together wrote over 60 percent of the New Testament?

In addition to what Paul said about Luke, we have the things Luke said about himself. The book of Acts contains numerous references to the author being part of the story and part of the action. We typically refer to those passages as the "we" sections. In some significant moments Luke was part of making the history he would later write about. For instance, he was with the mission team that went into Europe carrying the gospel there for the first time. Luke helped teach and baptize the first convert on European soil (Acts 16:10-17). He apparently stayed in Philippi after the first few converts came to Christ, presumably to disciple them. We might even say Luke was the pastor of the growing group of first-generation Christians (Acts 20:6). Luke was also present when a young man was raised from the dead, so his discussions and reports of miracles were, in part, based on his own experiences (Acts 20:7-12). The "we" sections include a few other episodes that help paint a picture of a hero of the early church movement. Luke was an adventurer and a pioneer missionary present and participating when some of the most dramatic events of Christian history occurred.

Early Church Tradition

A man like Luke would be the topic of numerous conversations and remembrances among the faithful long after his life. As a result, we have information about him not found in Scripture but retained in the history of the church by some well-known ancient voices. Among them are Eusebius and Jerome. Eusebius, born barely two hundred years after the books of Luke and Acts were completed, was a prominent and prolific historian and theologian from Caesarea, Israel, who wrote the first detailed history of Christianity from the time of the apostles.[6] Jerome was a linguist and Bible translator best known for the Latin Vulgate, a translation of nearly the entire Bible.[7] Both of these respected ancient Christian scholars taught that Luke was a native of Antioch, Syria, which is in the modern nation of Turkey.[8]

If that is correct, it might suggest Luke's connection to the apostle Paul if they came into contact during Paul and Barnabas's ministry in that busy city. We can only speculate about Luke's connection to Paul in Antioch, but it fits the timeline of the "we" sections of Acts, which do not begin until after the launch of the Gentile mission from Antioch (Acts 13).

Finally, we want to know if Luke was a Gentile. It has been common to assume Luke was a Gentile for some time. [9] In recent years, however, that assumption has been seriously questioned by some New Testament scholars. [10]

Luke is a fascinating and yet somewhat unsung hero in the Christian life. He traveled with Paul and not only chronicled early Christian history but made history too! We may wish we had more information about Luke the man, but his writings are his most important contribution, and we should become increasingly familiar with them as we attempt to find progress in the Christian life and power for our witness.

---

[1] Gordon D. Fee and Douglas Stuart, *How to Read the Bible for All Its Worth* (Grand Rapids, MI: Zondervan, 1982), 111.

[2] Simon J. Kistemaker, *The Gospels in Current Study*, 2nd ed. (Grand Rapids, MI: Baker Book House, 1972), 104–5.

[3] David E. Garland, *Luke*, Exegetical Commentary on the New Testament (Grand Rapids, MI: Zondervan, 2011), 56.

[4] Kistemaker, *The Gospels in Current Study*, 113.

[5] Ibid.

[6] Michael Walsh, ed., *Dictionary of Christian Biography* (Collegeville, MN: Liturgical Press, 2001), 441.

[7] Ibid., 656.

[8] Trent C. Butler, et al., eds., *Holman Bible Dictionary* (Nashville: Holman Bible Publishers, 1991), 899.

[9] Robert H. Gundry, *A Survey of the New Testament*, rev. ed. (Grand Rapids, MI: Zondervan, 1981), 96.

[10] Two Baptist professors, David L. Allen and David E. Garland, in separate works have recently challenged the Gentile background of Luke. See David L. Allen, *Lukan Authorship of Hebrews* (Nashville: B&H Publishing, 2010) and Garland, *Luke*, Exegetical Commentary of the New Testament.

Chapter 1

The Jesus Agenda

Luke 4:16-30

I saw Jesus at the grocery store. As I inched through the checkout line, there He was, imagined by Rembrandt, on the cover of a monthly magazine. I couldn't resist; I had to buy it. When magazines have Jesus on the cover, their sales go through the roof! One report says He can boost sales by as much as 45 percent.[1] Jesus has graced the covers of the most famous newsmagazines in America two or three times a year for more than half a century. It's a certainty that no one else who lived two thousand years ago has ever been so frequently seen on magazine stands.

Jesus is, by most accounts, the most well-known person in history. He is loved and celebrated throughout the world. On and off Broadway, in current movies, and on television, Jesus is still a Superstar. More than two billion people worldwide identify themselves as followers of Jesus, approximately one-third of the world's population. And in spite of current persecution, competing religious ideologies, and the renaissance of theistic skepticism on a popular level, more than seventy thousand people from all over the world voluntarily convert to Jesus every day.[2]

On any given day images of Jesus can be seen on pithy bumper stickers, and dads display Him on T-shirts at the mall. He's ubiquitous in the unoriginal, religious clip art peppered daily throughout social media. More books have been written about Jesus than any other individual in history. As much as it may be offensive to His genuine followers to hear it stated this way, the evidence is conclusive: Jesus is a celebrity in America. As a result, the real message of Jesus may sometimes get lost or relegated to a place of secondary significance in the glare of Jesus's popular appeal.

Ironically, He had the same dilemma in His own town of Nazareth, Israel. In fact, He was the first resident in Nazareth's long, uneventful history who had gained any notoriety outside of local family histories and small-town gossip. That unwanted celebrity status almost cost Him His life one Sabbath morning in His hometown.

Jesus of Nazareth

Jesus wasn't born in Nazareth. He moved there as a young boy with his parents—Joseph and Mary, two well-known former residents who had both grown up in the isolated village but had left town a few years earlier.

Life in Nazareth was predictable when Jesus was growing up. The village was extremely small. The "city limits" were not measured in square miles but by hundreds of feet. Nazareth, at the time of Jesus, was probably no more than about ten acres, the rough equivalent of three city blocks in modern Manhattan in New York City. Houses were small, made from the abundance of rock everywhere, and were often built simply by making use of the hillside as a back wall. Some residents used the natural caves to create crude dwellings and merely constructed additional rooms, walls, and entrances around the natural lay of the land. There was nothing elaborate about construction in Nazareth, and everyone lived in close proximity, creating a kind of small, stony, common courtyard outside their front doors.

The entire town was built on a steep hillside; the soil was rocky and not as well suited for farming as the lush land around the Sea of Galilee, which lay approximately fifteen miles to the east at the base of winding mountain paths. Water was always an issue, with only a few springs known to have existed for the few isolated families who lived in Nazareth. Rainfall, therefore, was essential for life; and the meager total, roughly twenty-two inches annually, fell mostly in the winter and had to be preserved. The porous rock upon which the little village was built allowed for construction of underground cisterns to hold water.

Life was never easy for the people of Nazareth. Medical support was limited and probably not much more sophisticated than home remedies. Due to the high mortality rate related to childbirth, women rarely outlived their husbands, and everyone in the family worked to live, barely struggling above subsistence their entire lives.

Fortunately, every week they received a brief reprieve from their labor. The social center of the tiny community was their synagogue. The Sabbath service was a welcome break from the endless hours of work. It was an occasion to worship God and an opportunity to converse with other families and reacquaint themselves with their community. The synagogue of Nazareth was small, but people attended regularly. Jesus Himself attended regularly throughout his childhood into adulthood. In a community as small as Nazareth, fewer than fifty adult men may have gathered on the Sabbath, each intimately familiar with the lives of the others.

That's one reason, when Jesus came back home to Nazareth, He stood out in the synagogue, even though He had attended hundreds of times before. He had left a few months earlier, and the reports about His ministry in the towns around the Sea of Galilee had ignited the curiosity of His old friends in Nazareth. The older men and all of His contemporaries had always known Jesus was different. From an early age He showed a strong interest in the ministries carried out at the temple in Jerusalem, and He was keenly adept at comprehending the teaching of the rabbis, had an unusual aptitude for Scripture, and always seemed unnaturally mature for His age (2:46-47).

Everyone in town liked Jesus when He was growing up (v. 52), but what they had heard about His ministry since He had left town was exceptional. Nothing like it had ever occurred. The entire region was talking about Him and His teaching ministry in synagogues all over Galilee (4:14-15). So, when He came back, He was a celebrity, and that new and unwanted status fueled passionate feelings about Him that moved from curiosity to violence in a matter of moments. Few people who ever encountered Jesus were emotionally neutral about Him.

Jesus Teaches in the Synagogue

Every four years in America a president is elected, and on the day He is sworn in, he gives his inaugural address. In that speech the new president lays out his agenda to the nation. He explains himself, his hopes, and his plans.

When Jesus went back to Nazareth, He was there to

formally present the "inaugural address" of His mission. He laid out His plans and clarified His agenda. That day did not end well.

The day began full of promise. Jesus returned from His first preaching mission, following forty days of fasting and temptation in the Judean desert, full of the Holy Spirit (vv. 1-15). It was His lifelong custom to attend the synagogue service in Nazareth every Sabbath (v. 16). As He entered, He took a seat, and when it was appropriate, He stood to read.

In other places in the New Testament, we witness the custom of inviting visiting teachers to contribute to the service (Acts 13:14-16). The scene that unfolds in Nazareth is not only the first description in the New Testament of a synagogue's order of service; it's the oldest account found anywhere.[3] It is also the first time Luke pulls back the curtain to give us a glimpse at the kind of message Jesus was teaching in the synagogues.

The Old Testament was held in the highest regard in the synagogues. Someone was routinely chosen for the privilege of handling the scrolls and making certain they were delivered to the rabbi when it was time to read. The scrolls were large, and their size and the special cabinet where they were stored conveyed their importance. It was a badge of honor for a synagogue to have all the scrolls. They were a "people of the Book." The scroll of Isaiah was handed to Jesus. It's not clear if receiving that scroll was by "chance" or if Jesus requested it. Or a third option may be in play. If the Scripture was read in a multiyear cycle of assigned readings, Jesus may have deliberately chosen this Sabbath to be in Nazareth to officially launch His public ministry. In any event, the reading fit perfectly with Jesus's intended purpose for being there that day.

The synagogue design was not exactly the same in every town, but there were similarities. Men sat around the sides of the room so everyone could easily see, hear, and participate. A table on which to rest the large scrolls was front and center.

The attendant handed Jesus the scroll, and Luke focuses attention on the process of unrolling the scroll and Jesus glancing over it to find an exact spot in the text (Luke 4:17). Luke is clearly creating a literary moment that draws the reader intimately into the action. We can almost feel ourselves slightly holding our breath as Jesus unrolls the scroll and silently looks it over before He suddenly begins to read.

The primary text He chooses is Isaiah 61:1-2, and Jesus adds a reading from Isaiah 58:6 but reads these passages as if they are one. In this way He shows the relationship between the two passages but also makes His own mission clearer.

The Anointing of the Spirit (v. 18)

The first thing Jesus makes clear is His relationship to the Holy Spirit. In the mind of Jesus, He has been sent by the Spirit to complete a work. No discrepancy is noted here, either in the words of Jesus or in the mind of Luke the Gospel writer, between the fact that Jesus was sent and anointed by the Spirit (v. 18) and the fact that in other places He gives God the Father praise for sending Him on mission (10:21-22). For Jesus, the leadership of the Spirit is the means by which God accomplishes His work through Christ.

As a Gospel writer, Luke is exceptionally interested

in displaying the activity of the Holy Spirit in the story of Jesus. For instance, he tells us John the Baptist would "be filled with the Holy Spirit" before his birth (1:15). The angel informed Mary "the Holy Spirit" would be the power that causes the virgin conception to occur (v. 35). Then Elizabeth was "filled with the Holy Spirit" when she saw Mary (v. 41). Later Zechariah was "filled with the Holy Spirit and prophesied" (v. 67).

Next we meet a man in the temple named Simeon. Luke tells us "the Holy Spirit was upon him" (2:25). Simeon had previously received special revelation from the Holy Spirit (v. 26), and he entered the temple "in the Spirit" (v. 27). When John the Baptist emerges on the scene, about the age of thirty, he promised the coming of a mighty figure, "the straps of whose sandals" John felt unworthy to untie, who would "baptize you with the Holy Spirit and fire" (3:16). When Jesus did come to the Jordan to be baptized by John, an incredible event occurred after the baptism. While Jesus was praying "the heavens were opened, and the Holy Spirit descended on him in bodily form, like a dove" (vv. 21-22).

Luke doesn't stop at the baptism. His fascination with the Holy Spirit's ministry continued with "Jesus, full of the Holy Spirit" as He returned from the baptism and was then "led by the Spirit in the wilderness" (4:1). Finally, after forty days of fasting, prayer, and spiritual warfare, "Jesus returned in the power of the Spirit to Galilee" (v. 14).

So it should come as no surprise to the reader at this point when Jesus publicly inaugurated His ministry by acknowledging, "The Spirit of the Lord is upon Me, / because He has anointed Me" (v. 18).

What is the anointing of the Holy Spirit? What did Jesus mean? We must start with what Jesus and His first hearers understood by the word *anointing*. The obvious frame of reference for Jesus's understanding of anointing is found in the Old Testament, especially since He was quoting an Old Testament passage.

The earliest references to the concept of anointing occur in the writings of Moses. It means to pour or smear a liquid onto a person or thing. In Genesis, Jacob "anointed" a stone by pouring oil upon it (Gen. 28:18; 31:13). The reason he did so was to commemorate the fact that at that spot he had encountered God. The anointing of the stone was a way to dedicate the place to God. That single action with a rock actually gets at the purpose behind anointing in the Old Testament. The same word is used for the process of anointing the priests' clothing so it would be ordained and consecrated for God's purposes (Ex. 28:41). When the word was applied to a person, it often involved pouring oil on the head, demonstrating the person was dedicated to God. The anointing of Aaron, for instance, was a sign of consecration and the conferring of the authority to act in the role of priest. Later, when Samuel was assigned the task of finding a new king for Israel, David was anointed in the same manner, with oil poured on his head (1 Sam. 16:13). When David was anointed with the oil, the Spirit of God "rushed upon David from that day forward." A similar thing occurred when Saul was anointed, and the Spirit of God caused him to "be turned into another man" (1 Sam. 10:6).

The anointing of priests and kings in the Old Testament prepared the men in every way possible to function in their new roles of responsibility. As a result of the anointing with oil, they had the spiritual authority, as well as the spiritual empowerment, to do the task God wanted them to do. Therefore, when Jesus claimed to be anointed by the Holy Spirit, He was using the word in the same way it had been commonly understood in the past. For Jesus, to be anointed by the Spirit meant He had been given the authority to act as God's Ambassador to accomplish whatever God had sent Him to do. He did not require additional credentials or authorization from anyone. God's Spirit had anointed Him. In addition to being authorized to serve, He was also empowered to serve. The "oil" used was the Spirit Himself, and the One who anointed Him was not a prophet but God Himself.

The work of the Holy Spirit will continue to stand out in Luke's Gospel as a major theme. In fact, a comparison to the other Synoptics puts Luke's focus on the Spirit in perspective. Mark and Matthew combined mention the Holy Spirit eighteen times, while Luke mentions the Spirit no fewer than seventeen times in his Gospel and in the book of Acts at least another seventy times![4]

What Jesus Was Anointed to Do (vv. 18-19)

Jesus had a heart for the oppressed, the forgotten, and the overlooked of culture. He was Spirit anointed to "proclaim good news to the poor" (v. 18). His church would later grow exponentially across the Roman Empire because the poor and the impoverished responded so readily to the message of the Gospel (1 Cor. 1:26-28).

Jesus was also anointed to "proclaim liberty to the captives." He saw people as captive and in need of liberation, to such a degree it would require the incarnation of God into human flesh and later His atoning death to accomplish their freedom. We must be much more captive to sin than we confess if our freedom requires God's Son to open our prison doors!

All of the Gospels describe Jesus's healing the blind (Matt. 20:29-34; Mark 10:46-52; Luke 18:35-43; John 9:1-7). Luke puts the miraculous healing ministry at the forefront by reminding his readers of Jesus's own words regarding healing blindness. In our culture of quality health care, eye surgeries, stylish glasses, and disposable contact lenses, it is hard to imagine a society where none of those things existed. Jesus came to give sight to the blind in a spiritual sense as well, but we cannot discount His promise of physical healing. The promise of sight was an extraordinary hope for the ancient world. We should see, in this use of an Old Testament reference to the healing ministry of the Messiah, a broad prediction of all of the healing miracles Jesus performed.

The focus of ministry to the dispossessed is a key theme in the book of Luke, which will occur again and again. In fact, later in Luke, Jesus would tell John the Baptist's disciples to inform John in prison about the Lord's ministry to the blind, the lame, lepers, and the deaf and that "the poor have good news preached to them" (7:22). Obviously, the ministry to outcasts, the poor, and the otherwise overlooked of society was a major focus for Jesus, and Luke returns to highlight that theme repeatedly.

Finally, Jesus came to "proclaim the year of the Lord's favor" (4:19). This hopeful message was in stark contrast to the Pharisees who refused to support the popular ministry of John the Baptist, even though the common people were enthralled by him (7:30), and they were disgusted by Jesus's friendship with "sinners" (15:1-2). Jesus's message was hope and salvation while His hearers were more accustomed to stern condemnation from the religious authorities of their day.

The Response to Jesus (vv. 20-30)

As a preacher I have learned to expect different reactions from congregations hearing the same message, but what Jesus experienced after His message in Nazareth was extreme. The first response of the congregation in Nazareth appears to be shock as they sat in silence staring at Jesus (v. 20). It's as if they didn't know what to say, or perhaps they were waiting to hear from Him. He broke the tension by declaring the prophecy of Isaiah had been fulfilled that day (v. 21). Apparently they did not fully grasp what Jesus meant, because they started affirming Him and one another but minimizing Him by referring to Him as "Joseph's son." To them it was a way of claiming Him as one of their own, but they clearly missed the bigger picture of His identity.

Jesus provoked their provincialism by reminding them of Old Testament examples of Gentiles who received God's blessing while Jews were overlooked (vv. 23-27). Immediately upon hearing these challenges, the men Jesus had known all of His life turned on Him and unsuccessfully tried to kill Him! (vv. 28-30).

Luke uniquely demonstrated that the ministry of Jesus will never be captive to a single people group or any perspective that ignores His divine authority or identity. The

"Jesus" agenda includes the entire world, and nothing can stop Him from fulfilling His mission!

For Memory and Meditation

"The Spirit of the Lord is upon me,
> because he has anointed me
> to proclaim good news to the poor.
He has sent me to proclaim liberty to the captives
> and recovering of sight to the blind,
> to set at liberty those who are oppressed,
to proclaim the year of the Lord's favor."

(Luke 4:18-19)

---

[1] David Gilson, "Jesus, What a Cover," *Mother Jones,* December 2005, https://www. motherjones.com/media/2005/12/jesus-newsweek-time-magazine-covers/.

[2] Jeremiah J. Johnston, *Unimaginable: What Our World Would Be Like without Christianity* (Grand Rapids, MI: Bethany House, 2017), 196.

[3] Robert H. Stein, *Luke*, The New American Commentary (Nashville: B&H Publishing Group, 1992), 155.

[4] Ibid., 47.

Chapter 2

Women and Children First

Luke 1:5-66

It may seem strange, but the facts are irrefutable. The closer we look, the more we see evidence that Luke wrote the birth narrative of Jesus from a woman's point of view. What do I mean? Luke's in-depth analysis of the birth narrative of Jesus puts women and their children at the forefront of the story. He tells the story by deliberately allowing the details of Christ's birth to unfold from the voices of the women closest to it.

Consider this: the first two chapters of Luke's Gospel have a combined total of 152 verses. Of those, women are the center of the activity, are in conversation with one another or God, or are being spoken to or described in no fewer than fifty-nine verses, almost 40 percent of the two chapters. When we isolate chapter 1, it is an even higher percentage of the action, with women at the center of the story in at least forty-two of the eighty verses, slightly more than half the chapter! When you add conversations about children, the percentages of the material devoted to both women and children skyrocket.

Luke was a historian focused on compiling the facts about Jesus from eyewitness accounts, and when reading the first two chapters, we can't help wondering if one of those eyewitnesses might have been Mary herself! While we have no way of knowing for certain, one thing we do know is that much of the material highlighting the prominent role of women and children in Luke's introduction is so personal only Mary could have been the original source for it, even if Luke did not interview her personally.

The Roman Empire at the time of Christ's birth may have enslaved women and treated wives like property, but in God's kingdom women were central to the story of God's purposes in the earth. Luke, more than any other Gospel writer, highlights the significant contributions of women in the life of the early church.

Introducing Elizabeth and John the Baptist (vv. 5-45)

All four Gospels introduce John the Baptist at the beginning of their narratives, but only Luke mentions his mother, Elizabeth.[1] In fact, Elizabeth is mentioned nowhere else in the Bible and, along with her husband Zechariah, is remembered for her personal devotion to God, her righteousness, and her habit of "walking blamelessly in all the commandments and statutes of the Lord" (v. 6). Scripture does not describe a faithful Jewish woman in more commendable terms.

Like Old Testament stories of God's intervention into the lives of other women who could not conceive a child, Elizabeth's conception is presented as a miracle on par with the miracles experienced by Isaac's mother, Sarah; Samuel's mother, Hannah; and Samson's mother, Manoah (Gen. 21:2; 1 Sam. 1:20; Judg. 13:2-3). Each of those Old Testament miracles led to the births of powerful leaders who advanced the causes of God and His people. The birth narrative of

John the Baptist is no exception. Of course, the real focus will ultimately land on the unprecedented, miraculous, virginal conception of the Savior, Jesus. But Luke is intentionally telling the story to build to that climax, as Joel B. Green points out: "The dominant feature on the literary landscape of Luke 1:5–2:52 is the point-by-point parallelism between John and Jesus."[2] The intentional similarities, however, are not meant to be "a juxtaposition of equals. Repeatedly the balance is tipped in favor of Jesus, so that we are left with no doubt as to who is the preeminent of the two children."[3]

The action surrounding the two births begins in Jerusalem. A priest from a town in Judah, so small it was not significant enough to identify, is preparing for a once-in-a-lifetime ministry in the temple. His name is Zechariah, and early in the narrative he is literally muted. His wife, Elizabeth, will become prominent in the unfolding drama. While it sometimes occurs, it is nevertheless rare in Scripture to find a biblical author so intent on establishing the highly desirable pedigree and exceptional spiritual qualifications of a female character like we find when we are introduced to Elizabeth. Yet, throughout Luke's Gospel (and Acts), women like Elizabeth are highlighted and held up as examples of the godly life. In this notable instance Luke is determined to demonstrate that Elizabeth was descended from Moses's brother, Aaron, so that, like her husband, she was from the direct genealogical line of the Hebrew priests. Priests like Zechariah were allowed to marry women outside the priestly class, but marrying a daughter of a priest added the highest credibility to their status and insured the sons of their union would be imminently qualified to follow in the footsteps of the priesthood.

Added to Zechariah and Elizabeth's Jewish pedigree is the exemplary testimony of their personal devotion to God and strict adherence to Jewish practice. They were "righteous before God, walking blamelessly in all the commandments and statutes of the Lord" (1:6). Zechariah and Elizabeth were the ancient Israeli equivalent of a "power couple," and Luke allows no distinction between their qualifications based on gender. They both have everything a Jewish family would aspire to, with the exception of one glaring, dramatic, missing element. It's the emptiness in their lives that sets up the narrative plotline Luke is weaving. What they don't have will create space for a miracle.

Luke, the master storyteller, immediately presents us with an insurmountable dilemma. Elizabeth is "barren" (physically incapable of conceiving a child). To add insult to misery, even if she had been physically capable of bearing a child, by the time we meet her she is too old—past the age possible for becoming a mother. This detail prepares us for the miracle to follow and draws us into the private suffering of this elderly couple who face their declining years with an empty home, absent of the joy of children and grandchildren. But God is good, and He is able to do more than we can imagine and intervenes when conventional wisdom says the time has passed, the door has closed, and all hope is lost.

Inside the holy place in the temple where a priest might never have the opportunity to serve during his entire life, Zechariah, who was only privileged to be in that esteemed space because he had been chosen by a random lottery, is offering incense on the altar as a symbol of perpetual prayer. No less than Gabriel, the messenger angel of God, appears in those close quarters assuring Zechariah that the couple's lifelong prayer to have a child has been heard, and God is going to miraculously allow Elizabeth to bear the couple's son, whom they are to name John. The section ends with Zechariah unable to speak and Elizabeth in hiding.

It's an almost humorous conclusion to what started as a tragic story of heartbreak. The priest can't even whisper, and his wife is privately shielding herself from public speculation and protecting her health and her unborn son. God has done the impossible in an unexplainable way. He has moved the old couple away from center stage and back to an anonymity even more isolated than the one they knew before we met them earlier in the retelling of their drama. In spite of what God has graciously done, they can't say a word about it to anyone! They will soon slip off the pages of history never to be heard of again, leaving us plenty of unanswered questions about how they raised the miracle child; if, in fact, they did at all. Or due to their old age, perhaps they sent him away to be raised by others in much the same way Hannah did with young Samuel (v. 80).

What happened to them after the birth of the baby is unknown, but we will see them one more time before they disappear from the pages of Scripture. First, however, we have to meet another woman living about a hundred miles north in the insignificant, hillside Jewish village of Nazareth.

Mary (vv. 26-56)

The most unforgettable miracle in history occurred in one of the most forgettable places on earth. Nazareth today is a fairly large, busy Arab town in northern Israel with a population made up of Muslims and Christians and is visited by Holy Land travelers year-round. However, when Mary was a young, single girl, Nazareth was a tiny Jewish village with a population of maybe three hundred people and probably fewer. Rising nearly sixteen hundred feet above sea level at its highest point, Nazareth is considerably higher in the distant hills than the well-known towns surrounding the Sea of Galilee, which is about seven hundred feet below sea level (the lowest freshwater lake on earth). Nazareth is approximately ninety miles northwest of Jerusalem and about fifteen miles west of the Sea of Galilee. In terms of culture, Nazareth was a world away from the busy populations in Jerusalem and the commercial fishing industry around the Sea of Galilee. Nazareth was so small and unimportant it isn't even mentioned in the Old Testament. As a result, it had no prophetic significance, which led one early follower of Jesus to wonder, "Can anything good come out of Nazareth?" (John 1:46).

For modern readers, Nazareth is a place with tremendous emotional attachment and sentimental value because we know Jesus grew up there; but for the Jews of Jesus's day it was an unlikely, rural, out-of-the-way, backward community of inexpensive, rugged hovels, with limited natural water sources and a few families of working-class peasants. No one was looking for miracles coming out of Nazareth.

Nazareth, we learn from Luke, was the hometown of both Mary and Joseph. Only two Gospels tell the birth story, and only Luke specifically tells us Nazareth was their original home. Matthew introduces us to Mary and Joseph without specifying where they live and never mentions any location until Jesus is born in Bethlehem (Matt. 1:18–2:1).

Since Luke tells us Joseph and Mary are from Nazareth, we can reasonably assume they must have known each other for most of their lives. In an isolated, mountain village with limited water sources and a population of fewer than three hundred people and forty families, virtually everyone would have been familiar with one another. It is remarkable, given his prominence in Matthew's version of the birth story, how little Joseph is mentioned in Luke's narrative since he is credited with being the link to King David (Matt. 1:16). He never speaks and is scarcely spoken to. No angels talk to him, he doesn't have any dreams, and he doesn't need to be convinced of the miraculous birth. He is a minor character in the background of the story with the spotlight on Mary who occupies a much larger role.

When Mary was confronted by the angel Gabriel, six months had passed since Elizabeth conceived. Mary was alone somewhere in Nazareth when the angel gave her the news. She was understandably "troubled" by the message of the angel and the significance of the message. As is usual in angelic visitations in Scripture, the angel assures her she has nothing to fear and in an economical three verses informs her she is to be the mother of the Son of God, who will occupy the throne of David's kingdom as the Jewish Messiah. Mary receives the overall message with an almost naive simplicity, more concerned with how it will happen than with the enormous implications of the angelic message.

The angel does not perceive her question as an example of doubt. Instead, she is genuinely interested in how the conception would transpire since she is an unmarried virgin. Earlier in the chapter Zechariah was penalized for questioning the angel's message (Luke 1:18), but Mary receives a direct answer to her simple question. She is told the Holy Spirit will act as the agent of God's power and would "overshadow" her, guaranteeing the baby would be "holy." The angel insisted the baby would be the "Son of God" (vv. 34-35).

Mary received an additional assurance when she was informed that her elderly relative, Elizabeth, who was previously unable to bear children, was now expecting as well. Luke is telling the birth stories of John the Baptist and Jesus from the vantage point of the women by bringing Elizabeth back into the story.

Luke's larger point is located in the concluding statement of the angel, "For nothing will be impossible with God" (v. 37). Mary humbly and immediately accepted the "impossible" blessing given to her.

The same God who worked in an "impossible" and almost clandestine way in the lives of women who would normally be overlooked can work a miracle in your life as well. An elderly woman with no children or grandchildren and a young, single girl in a rural, mountain village were not on anyone's short list to attract attention from the surrounding culture. Perhaps that's why God chose them. They were representative of the quiet multitude of unnoticed people of faith who experience miracles without recognition and blessings without notoriety. They remind us God never forgets His people and showers favor wherever He finds faith and people of prayer.

Mary and Elizabeth (vv. 39-66)

As soon as Mary learned of Elizabeth's miracle, she "arose and went with haste into the hill country" (v. 39). Luke doesn't concern himself with explanations about how the young, single girl managed the nearly ninety-mile journey. Her action speaks for itself. Mary, in spite of her youthfulness, is determined and self-reliant. Her self-determination draws the focus of the narrative to her once again as she moves with "haste" (the Greek word is *spoude*, from which we get our word *speed*). Mary was the beneficiary of a miracle like none before, and she wasted no time taking bold action and acting in faith.

Once Mary arrived at the home of her relatives—it is called Zechariah's house, but the old priest is never mentioned in this scene—what transpired was only between the women and their unborn babies. Luke highlights again the spiritual depth of Elizabeth by pointing out that when she saw Mary she was "filled with the Holy Spirit" (v. 41). Presumably the baby in the womb was also filled with the Spirit at this time, although it is not explicitly stated. Instead, it is probably inferred, based on the prophecy in verse 15 that the child would be "filled with the Holy Spirit even from his mother's womb." The ministry of the Holy Spirit is obvious throughout Luke and Acts, but the first time Luke uses the phrase "filled with the Holy Spirit" to refer to an individual it concerns Elizabeth (v. 41).

Elizabeth makes an incredible statement regarding Mary and her unborn baby. She prophetically refers to Mary as "the mother of my Lord" (v. 43). The angel had only spoken to Mary about the virgin conception of Jesus a few days earlier. From a typical, physical observation no one could have known Mary was expecting a baby within a week of conception—not even Mary. In addition, for godly Elizabeth to declare the microscopic embryo inside the virgin's womb as her "Lord" was either one of the great declarations of faith or blasphemy! Clearly, Luke sees it as a Spirit-empowered prophetic announcement.

In response Mary erupts with a song of praise richly dense with Old Testament allusions and vocabulary (vv. 46-55). Mary was young and from an insignificant village, but she somehow had been immersed in Old Testament stories and prophecy, and her words form "a virtual collage of biblical texts."[4] What is also striking, in addition to her knowledge of the Old Testament, is her grasp of the geopolitical circumstances surrounding her at the moment. She demonstrated wisdom of comprehension as she masterfully wove abstract concepts together from a variety of biblical passages and applied them to her current circumstances.

One of the themes present in Mary's song of praise is God's faithfulness to His people. Mary refers to His "mercy" consistent "from generation to generation" (v. 50). She also praises God for remembering the "humble" and for being the One who "scattered the proud" (vv. 51-52). These themes of God's special care for the poor and weak and His refusal to indiscriminately honor the rich and proud dominate the book of Luke. In Mary, Luke found a powerful voice to launch his persistent theological emphasis.

Luke told Theophilus his intention was to write an "orderly account" after careful research, which demonstrates Luke wrote intentionally and intelligently. Luke intended to lay the groundwork for his story upon the foundation of multiple witnesses, including two women and their babies. He shows the women as Spirit filled, expertly knowledgeable in Scripture, outspoken, self-reliant, and godly in every way. Elizabeth and Mary are powerful voices for building his gospel.

Luke obviously includes additional witnesses in the birth narrative, including Zechariah and his impressive prophecy (vv. 67-79). The shepherds are also introduced only by Luke, and the angelic host that invited them into the story cannot be ignored in the unique telling of the birth story from Luke's perspective. It is an overstatement to say all the birth story of Jesus is based on women's activities, but it is equally incorrect to ignore the unparalleled way women played a role in one of the most famous stories in the world.

Luke shows through two strongly committed women that regardless of cultural norms or convention, God can and will use anyone to bring glory and others to Himself. He will even use us.

For Memory and Meditation

"And the virgin's name was Mary." (Luke 1:27)

---

[1] For more information about John the Baptist, see my book *The King and His Community* (Tigerville, SC: Auxano Press, 2013), chap. 2.

[2] Joel B. Green, *The Gospel of Luke,* The New International Commentary on the New Testament (New York: Wm. B. Eerdmans, 1997), 50.

[3] Ibid., 51.

[4] Ibid., 101.

Chapter 3

Jesus Calling

Luke 5:1-11

Things changed one day when I got followers. I got hundreds of them.

A friend of mine had convinced me to open a Twitter account, even though I had no idea why I should or how it worked. A few close friends followed me. Then one day, when I had about thirty followers, a famous megachurch pastor with more than a million Twitter followers followed me.

On a summer afternoon a few days later, I tweeted a thought, and the megachurch pastor retweeted my blurb and thanked me by name. That's the day my Twitter presence jumped because followers started storming in. People I didn't know and who didn't know me followed me because someone influential mentioned my name. In less than a day I went from thirty followers to more than three hundred! Followers poured in from Indonesia, Taiwan, California, Indiana, South Africa, Florida, Australia, Idaho, and numerous other places. On social media the name of the game is followers. That day I got ten times more followers than I had before. Nothing like it has ever happened since.

One morning, long before the relative superfluity of social media, on the busy shores of the Sea of Galilee, Jesus started building His far more substantive group of followers. Two sets of brothers, partners in a commercial fishing business, were among His first followers. While all four Gospels refer to His earliest disciples, in most cases by name, Luke provides unparalleled, behind-the-scenes information about the day Jesus called and starting getting followers.

The Setting of the Call (vv. 1-7)

It's been said there's no success without a successor, and it's clear from His call for followers Jesus never intended to do ministry alone. His followers became His closest friends who perpetuated His ministry after His death, attracting tens of thousands of new followers throughout the Roman Empire. And it all started with Jesus's calling.

The Sea of Galilee has multiple names, including the "Sea of Tiberius" (John 21:1) and the "lake of Gennesaret" (Luke 5:1). Although it is widely referred to in the Gospels and in modern vernacular as the Sea of Galilee, it isn't a *sea* at all. It is a freshwater lake fed mostly by the Jordan River.

Tiberius Caesar was the Roman emperor during a part of Jesus's life. When Jesus was in His early twenties, King Herod Antipas, son of Herod the Great, built a town on the western shore of the Sea of Galilee and named it Tiberius, in a gesture of political deference to the emperor. As a result, the lake was sometimes referred to as the sea or lake of Tiberius.

Luke referred to the lake as Lake Gennesaret, based on its Old Testament name the "Sea of Chinnereth" (Josh. 13:27). The Hebrew word *Chinnereth* (sometimes also known as *Kinnereth*) and the Greek word *Gennesaret* both refer to the shape of the lake, which resembles a popular musical instrument, the harp or *kinor* in Hebrew. The harp-shaped Sea of Galilee, with its roughly thirteen mile length and its wide northern shore, stretching about eight miles east to west, narrows dramatically (like a harp) at its southern tip, tapering to less than two miles as it empties into the Jordan River, meandering down toward the Dead Sea.

The Sea of Galilee has always been filled with a variety of edible small fish, which allowed a flourishing commercial fishing industry to prosper. If a fisherman could buy enough boats and hire enough laborers, he could make an impressive living, allowing him eventually to have multiple houses, land and property, and multiple employees. Commercial fishing on the Sea of Galilee could make a hardworking, determined man wealthy, relatively speaking. From a composite portrait of Simon Peter, drawn from numerous data points scattered throughout the four Gospels, he appears to be that kind of man.

Jesus was teaching beside the Sea of Galilee early one morning when He noticed two boats at the shoreline, with fishermen busy with their work. The area around the lake where Peter's fishing business took place was heavily populated, and the teaching ministry of Jesus had attracted a crowd so large people were pushing and shoving and becoming potentially unruly. So Jesus got into one of the boats and asked its owner, Simon, later known as Peter, to push away from the shore so Jesus could continue teaching the large crowd without being overwhelmed by their aggressive demeanor. Being in the boat also allowed Jesus to be more easily heard, as the lake sits in an acoustically enhancing, natural bowl-shaped amphitheater, surrounded by high hills, including the Golan Heights on the northeast shore.

After the teaching had ended and the crowd, presumably, had wandered away, Jesus seemed to want to reward the boat owner for his hospitality by advising him where to cast his nets for an additional catch of fish. Simon's response was somewhere between reluctance and irritation. Commercial fishermen like Simon fished through the night on the Sea of Galilee. In the mornings they began the process of cleaning and repairing their equipment and processing the fish. The night before had been unproductive. Astoundingly, they hadn't caught a single fish. The only thing they had managed to do was tear their nets.

Simon and his partners were night fishermen who began fishing at sundown and stopped at sunrise so the fish could not see the nets. The popular image of the Israeli fisherman casting a small handheld net is probably not the way a large, professional fishing crew made the most of their time and efforts. Instead, they lowered extremely large, linen nets, probably measuring more than a hundred feet in circumference, into the deep, dark water. The nets were weighted around the edges so they slowly closed as they sank, capturing whatever fish they surrounded. The fishing crew then dragged the nets back into the boats, and they continued the process through the night. It could be lucrative, but it was physically demanding, backbreaking work.

The nets were an essential piece of equipment for fishing. Since they were constantly dragging across the rocky bottom of the lake, they inevitably got snagged and torn. It was one of the occupational hazards associated with the fisherman's career. Repairing and restitching huge, cumbersome nets was a tedious, daily routine in the fishing business. Because they were linen, they had to be cleaned daily to remove the seaweed and algae that grew in the warm lake, or they would quickly rot. The repair and cleaning were all done by hand, as soon as they had emptied the fish on the shore at daylight.[1] Unfortunately, the monotonous, time-intensive job also had to be done when they hadn't caught a thing.

Simon and his team were busy with those chores when Jesus arrived (Luke 5:2). No imagination is needed to guess how the business owners felt that morning. They had worked all night, as they did year-round, and now they were busy with the exhausting process of repairs and cleaning, even though their best efforts had turned up nothing. Into that frustrating scene Jesus, a man from a mountain village unrelated to the drudgery and challenges of the fishing business, calmly suggested they push out into deeper waters and let down their nets one more time (v. 4). They had just finished cleaning the nets, and exposing them to the water and the rocky lake bottom again would mean cleaning and, potentially, repairing them again. The fishermen were professionals. They knew fish wouldn't swim into nets they could see in clear water with the morning sun shining down. The request was ludicrous from an exhausted professional fisherman's perspective. What the fisherman could not know at that moment was that Jesus was drawing His own net around Simon.

The Initial Response to the Call (vv. 4-8)

The dialogue between Jesus and Simon out on the Sea of Galilee that morning is a case study of a man's unwillingness to follow the Lord's leadership and His undeterred patience insisting we do. The detail that makes this scene so provocative and universally common to our experience is that Simon had a reasonable and informed point of view. He was an expert on fishing those waters. He had "home court advantage" in this debate. That's how it always seems to us when we are convinced by all our previous experience to defend our position, in spite of the dilemma created when Jesus plainly calls us to follow an alternate path that makes no sense to us. It's hard to trust a plan that appears to be unreasonable.

Admittedly, Simon agreed to drop the nets again, but he was reluctant and mildly argumentative. He wanted Jesus to understand that the Sea of Galilee was predictable and going back again would be meaningless. Simon reminded Jesus that he was only going along with His request as a favor. He subtly suggested that when the nets came back up empty, they would all know who was at fault for attempting such an ill-advised venture. "Master, we toiled all night and took nothing! But at your word I will let down the nets" (v. 5).

Simon's tendency to debate with Jesus or to attempt to advise Him was a habit Luke highlights throughout the Gospel. For instance, when a crowd was pressing in on Jesus as they walked along, a woman discreetly touched Jesus and received healing. No one noticed her, but Jesus felt power leave Him and asked who had touched Him. "When all denied it, Peter said, 'Master, the crowds surround you and are pressing in on you!'" (8:45).

Simon Peter felt a need to correct Jesus or wonder aloud at times if Jesus really understood the situation. Another time they were experiencing a miracle on a mountaintop as Moses and Elijah appeared to talk with Jesus. Peter, in an amazing display of shortsighted enthusiasm, came up with the idea of building tents for the visitors so they could all just stay on the mountain. His idea was so unfocused and wrongheaded, Luke had to acknowledge how foolish it was. "And as the men were parting from him, Peter said to Jesus, 'Master, it is good that we are here. Let us make three tents, one for you and one for Moses and one for Elijah'—not knowing what he said" (9:33).

Simon made a life out of making the wrong decisions in a big, unmistakable way! Yet Jesus wanted the outgoing, sometimes careless fisherman to help lead the ministry Jesus was building. So, when Simon complained about dropping the nets, Jesus let it pass. Simon would soon learn, for the first time, a lesson he would need to learn again a few times. Arguing with Jesus was useless. His plans are always best. It took Peter a while to learn that lesson. Perhaps there's still a little more time for all of us to learn it as well.

The Unexpected Catch (vv. 6-9)

There's an old saying about giving a person enough rope and he'll hang himself. Jesus may have allowed Simon Peter to experience a little of that old adage in the abundant catch of fish! Simon appears to be the leader of the business, and with ownership comes responsibility. He had partners; there were family connections; payrolls had to be met; quality controls had to be maintained; plans needed to be in place for the future; and an empty boatful of empty nets after a night of fishing was bad for morale and bad for the bottom line.

The Sea of Galilee today, like other bodies of water in

Israel, is shrinking. Demands on water continue to grow with the population, and the Sea of Galilee is still one of the main freshwater supplies for the nation. We know the lake was bigger in Jesus's time, but even today it has a depth of more than 140 feet. As Simon pushed away from the shore and into the deeper waters to let down his nets, they immediately began to fill with an unprecedented catch of fish. Others were in the boat with Jesus and Simon (v. 6), and one suspects there had been a few eye rolls and heavy sighs from the crew when Simon had originally agreed to fish in daylight hours. But all the doubt turned to exuberance when the catch of fish was bigger than any they had ever seen. There were so many fish, the freshly cleaned and repaired nets started to break under the weight of the fish. It was a fisherman's dream come true.

Simon looked at fish and saw profits! He called for the other boat in his little fleet to leave the shore and go out to the deep spot, alongside his boat, to help with this windfall of fish! When they arrived, presumably helmed by his partners James and his younger brother John, both boats started hauling in the catch, and the abundance of fish brought on board both fishing vessels was too much. Both fishing boats started to sink because they were loaded with so many fish.

Suddenly, Simon had a flash of spiritual clarity. He knew he was eyewitness to a miracle, and Jesus was eyewitness to greed and self-serving avarice. Simon had a tender heart and repented of his greed. He expressed shame and regret and "fell down at Jesus' knees, saying, 'Depart from me, for I am a sinful man, O Lord'" (v. 8).

In that moment Jesus knew He had gained a follower.

Having once witnessed what God is able to do—even when Simon himself was skeptical—the fisherman could never look at life on the Sea of Galilee the same way again. He had come to realize fully there is more to life than all your dreams coming true. Knowing the Lord and finding His will is greater every time. Besides that, Jesus had a historic catch in mind, bigger and better by far than anything Peter could catch in those big linen nets on the Sea of Galilee.

The Call to Start Over (vv. 10-11)

The city where I lived was the home, briefly, of the X Games, a multiday sporting event where the so-called "extreme sports" are played. Motocross races, mountain bike exhibitions giving young daredevils an opportunity to defy gravity and thrill fans, and skateboard competitions, attracting the best skateboarders in the world were just a few events performed by the athletic adrenalin junkies that entered the X Games. But three years into a four-year contract, the X Games pulled out of Austin. The problem, according to the general consensus, was the Austin summer heat! Even extreme athletes draw the line somewhere.

Some people live for the thrill of danger and extreme risk. We admire those young people but usually not enough to join them in their sport. Most people want something different from life than a constant adrenalin rush or the prospects of using a bicycle to turn a somersault twenty-five feet in the air with nothing but dirt or pavement beneath. No, we like to live vicariously through the X Games athletes. Most people want security, stability, assurance their job will be there tomorrow, and loved ones to come home to at the end of the day.

Change is inevitable in life. The more we stand to lose in the transition, the more difficult it is for us to give up the known for the unknown. You may be the opposite. Maybe you're an adrenalin junkie looking for the next thrill. If so, I applaud you, but most people want security, not risk.

That's why the call of Jesus is electrifying in its audacity. Jesus said to these men who owned businesses and homes and had wives and families, "Do not be afraid; from now on you will be catching men" (v. 10). His invitation was broad, not very specific, and used only metaphorical terms; but these men—Simon, James, John, and, presumably, Andrew, Simon's brother—did the unthinkable. "And when they had brought their boats to land, they left everything and followed him" (v. 11).

Can you imagine this? Huge nets, hundreds of fish, expensive boats, and all the equipment needed to be a success in the fishing business just sat there—abandoned on the shore with a small wave lapping against it while the former owners followed an itinerant Teacher and Miracle Worker into a life unknown.

Within three years that same fishing boat captain, who had marched away without a second thought from the biggest catch of his life, would stand in Jerusalem and proclaim the death and resurrection of Jesus to thousands of Jewish worshippers gathered for an annual feast. When he completed that message, three thousand people repented, believed the gospel, were baptized in a single day, and joined the same movement that had attracted him three years earlier (Acts 2:14-42).

What gives a person the willingness to start over? The answer seems trite and unsophisticated, but the simple answer is Jesus. He has called billions to a new life, and He continues to do so around the world today. Have you heard Him call you? Will you follow?

For Memory and Meditation

"And Jesus said to Simon, 'Do not be afraid; from now on you will be catching men.' And when they had brought their boats to land, they left everything and followed him." (Luke 5:10-11)

---

[1]David N. Bivin, "The Miraculous Catch: Reflections on the Research of Mendel Nun," *Jerusalem Perspective*, January 6, 2013, accessed January 16, 2018, https://www.jerusalemperspective.com/2644.

Chapter 4

Neighbors

Luke 10:29-37

Someone once said that peace is that rare moment when everybody stops to reload at once. Unfortunately, at times, that cynical view does not seem to be too far from the truth. All over the world we live with the threat of terrorism at airports, concerts, sporting events, or anywhere a large crowd of innocent people gather. As of this writing, nine nations are believed to have nuclear weapons.[1] The world is a dangerous place.

Frequently nations face the greatest hostility from the neighboring nations nearest to them. South Korea and North Korea are current examples. They are both small countries divided by a border of only 160 miles in length. But the worldview of the two governments and the lifestyles of the two people groups are diametrically opposed.

In previous generations we saw the same kind of differences exist between East Germany and West Germany. In American history our nation was once ripped into the United States and the Confederate States. Neighbors with shared pasts may sometimes have radically different ideas about the future.

These examples may help us put into perspective the hostility that existed for hundreds of years between Samaritans and Jews and understand why Jesus's story about a "good" Samaritan would have been met with stunned and even angry disbelief by most of the Jews who followed Him. Only Luke recounts the story we refer to as the parable of the good Samaritan. It is a further example of Luke's emphasis on Jesus's willingness to reach a world outside the Jewish family, especially those who were traditionally shunned. But more than that, it's a challenge to show mercy to whoever needs it.

Samaritans and Jews

Looking at a map to see where biblical Samaria was located can be helpful. Modern Israel is a small country. Its total length is less than the distance between Tampa and Miami. Samaria was in the middle of the nation, bordered on the east by the Jordan River and reaching as far west as the Mediterranean Sea. At the time of Jesus, the nation of Israel was geographically divided between Galilee in the north, Samaria in the center, and Judah in the south.

Hundreds of years of bad blood had developed between the Jews and their neighbors, the Samaritans. The Samaritans had Jewish ancestry and a modified version of the Jewish religion, but they also had ancestors from the nations of the Gentiles (Ezra 4:10). People living in Samaria had been Jewish, but after Assyria destroyed the Northern Kingdom of Israel, where Samaria was located, the Assyrians deported most of the Jews out of Samaria and brought other subjugated people groups in to repopulate the area. That's how the Samaritans became a mixed-race people group. The relatively few Jews left in the land intermarried with the Gentiles, which led to the new people group we know now as Samaritans. That ethnic complexity gave rise to tensions that were never resolved between the Jews and their neighbors in Samaria.

Animosities reached a boiling point on numerous occasions, but one prominent flare-up occurred when the Jewish leader Zerubbabel was building the second temple, after the end of the Babylonian captivity. The Babylonian captivity was an event that took place almost six hundred years before Christ, yet it dominates much of the Old Testament's focus and changed the ways the Jews practiced their faith. Examples of those changes were more fully developed by the time of the New Testament, including the importance of the synagogues, the rise of the Pharisees sect, and the importance of the rabbis.

Samaritans, by the time of Zerubbabel's rebuilding effort, were holding on to the first five books of the Old Testament as their Bible but had rejected the Wisdom Literature and the Prophets. The Samaritans were all descended from a mixed ethnic heritage, and this was at a time when the Jews were especially sensitive to the importance of unmixed Jewish bloodlines (Ezra 9–10). Consequently, when the Jews came back to Jerusalem after decades in Babylonian captivity, they were fiery in their opposition about allowing Samaritan assistance with the rebuilding of the temple. The Samaritans volunteered to help and were told publicly, "You have nothing to do with us in building a house to our God; but we alone will build a house to the LORD" (Ezra 4:3).

It got worse. The Samaritans built a rival temple on Mount Gerizim in Samaria. A little more than a hundred years before the birth of Christ, a Jewish general named John Hyrccanus rallied a mercenary army and rode to

Mount Gerizim and destroyed the Samaritan temple. The bloodshed and hatred between Jews and Samaritans kept the feud alive for hundreds of years.

By the time of Jesus, Jews were forbidden from speaking to Samaritans and were considered ceremonially unclean if they ate from a Samaritan dish (John 4:9). The neighborhood had become decidedly unneighborly.

The Reason for the Parable (vv. 25-29)

The phrase "gotcha journalism" may have been coined recently, but the concept of trying to trap a person in his or her own words has a long history! Religious leaders constantly tried to catch Jesus saying something that could discredit Him in the eyes of the common people. Repeatedly, however, Jesus's answers had the opposite effect.

An "expert in the law" (NIV) or "lawyer" in the New Testament was a biblical scholar, and one such lawyer attempted to "test" Jesus (v. 25). In other words, the lawyer had a "gotcha question." It seemed simple enough on the surface, "What must I do to inherit eternal life?" (NIV). What is not clear is how, and in how many ways, the religious leader planned to twist Jesus's potential answer into an unwinnable debate. The answer he got was probably unexpected: Jesus asked him a question in response. For those who have read the Gospels, Jesus's response is not surprising. He rarely answered a question directly but often asked a question in answer to a question.

So, in response to the lawyer's question about eternal life, Jesus simply asked the biblical expert how he would answer his own question from a biblical perspective. The man's answer about loving God and loving his neighbor demonstrated his expertise in biblical teaching. Jesus commended him for his answer and told him to go do it (vv. 27-28). The man was dissatisfied with Jesus's response and continued to probe, in hopes of sparking a debate. Since Jesus advocated loving our neighbors as ourselves, the lawyer seized on the potentially controversial aspect of the question and its answer.

Luke informs the reader that the man was seeking to "justify himself" by asking the seemingly harmless follow-up question, "Who is my neighbor?" (v. 29). The word *justify* is a common New Testament word, usually referring to righteousness. In this case it indicates the man felt outflanked by Jesus and was trying to regain his argument and perhaps save face. The word *neighbor* could merely mean any other person, a person nearby, or, in the Jewish mind, another Hebrew.

Israel was an occupied nation at the time of Christ, politically dominated by the Romans. Therefore, it was filled with Roman leaders and soldiers at all times. With the geographical proximity to the Samaritans, Jesus's answer could potentially stir up an argument. Most Jews wouldn't acknowledge Romans or Samaritans as neighbors. In fact, the Pharisees, who were leaders of the local synagogues and influential among the people, seemed reluctant even to claim all Jews as their neighbor (John 7:49).

The lawyer had accomplished phase one of his goal. He had publicly asked Jesus questions laced with intricate and subtle controversies built into any potential answer. Depending on how Jesus answered, phase two of the biblical scholar's plan would involve exploiting the responses to paint Jesus in a negative light in the minds of those who followed Him. If the lawyer was looking for an explosive response, he got more than he bargained for when Jesus successfully coaxed the lawyer to acknowledge publicly that a Samaritan could act better than a Jewish priest when confronted with a humanitarian crisis.

The Road to Jericho (vv. 30-37)

Jerusalem is about twenty-five hundred feet above sea level, and Jericho is about 850 feet below sea level, so the road to Jericho is mountainous and steep in places between the two cities, which are about fifteen miles apart. Jericho is northeast of Jerusalem. Americans tend to refer to places as "up north" or "down south." But in Israel, everything is "down" from Jerusalem, mostly based on elevation. Because the ancient road was a winding mountain path, it was isolated in spots and lent itself to dangerous and nearly defenseless areas where robberies and assaults could, and did, occur.

Jericho had played an important role in Israeli history since it was there General Joshua experienced a miracle of God. Forty years before the miracle, when Joshua was a young soldier, Moses had sent him, along with eleven others, on a clandestine mission to examine the promised land before the Israelites entered it. The twelve spies were to bring back a scouting report after their reconnaissance mission in order to prepare for the Israeli invasion.

Unfortunately the majority report was negative. The people of the land were tall and strong, and their cities had walls (Num. 13:28). Joshua was a minority voice who believed God would somehow deliver the impressive walled cities into the hands of the Israeli nation of wandering slaves. But his voice had been drowned out by the fearful and the faithless. Since Joshua was so confident God would give the fortified cities into the hands of the Israelites, the crowd decided unsuccessfully to kill him in order to silence his militant exuberance! (Num. 14:6-10)

After four decades the tables had turned, and young Joshua was the successor to Moses and was leading the next generation into the promised land their parents had refused to enter. Jericho was in the way of their progress.

One of the oldest continually inhabited cities on earth, Jericho, called "the City of Palms" (Deut. 34:3 NIV), was the first walled city the Israelites encountered as they entered the promised land. The walls were impressive and had protected the ancient city for longer than anyone could remember, but miraculously they "fell down flat" when God delivered the city to Joshua and his invading troops (Josh. 6:20).

As a result of our familiarity with the miracle of the walls of Jericho falling down, we may forget that the city was rebuilt and is still very real. Certainly for the people of Jesus's time, it was a well-known and important neighboring town.

Jesus's story, centering around an unfortunate Jewish traveler being mugged, beaten, and robbed on the road, would have made this parable extremely interesting and realistic to the first hearers. They must have wondered where He was headed with the story. It's virtually certain they could not have guessed!

The Parable (vv. 30-35)

We know nothing about the victim in the story of the good Samaritan, but we feel immediate sympathy for him. We presume his innocence because he was beaten by thieves and left to die. It's clear the villains of this story are the robbers, yet we know nothing about them either, and they quickly disappear from the story. When Jesus injects new characters into the story, the plot deepens in an unexpected way. The story is not about getting justice for the victim and judgment on the thieves. Jesus wants us to focus instead on who might help the poor man.

First, we are introduced to a Jewish priest. Priests were the ministers in the temple. They were an elite class of people descended from Aaron, Moses's brother, and the only people in the religion qualified to offer sacrifices in the temple. They were respected religious leaders. They spent their time occupied with the holiest of matters, and the average person would have considered them to be more ceremonially clean and right with God than other people.

The expectation, therefore, is the priest would do the right thing. He would help the poor man. But he didn't (v. 31).

Next, a Levite happened by. He, likewise, was a religious leader. Levites, like priests, were descendants of Levi but from a different branch of the family tree and, therefore, not qualified to serve in the priesthood. In spite of this, they were still official ministers responsible for the organizational details of daily temple activities and rituals. Certainly the Levite would help the victim. Yet, like the priest, the Levite "when he came to the place and saw him, passed by on the other side" (v. 32).

Jesus gives no reason the religious leaders avoided helping the man, but He chose to cast them in a negative light in order to create tension and contrast in the action. That contrast comes when He mentioned the Samaritan.

The Samaritan is not referred to in Jesus's story as "good." His kind and responsive actions have earned him the title "good Samaritan" over the centuries. It's interesting to note here how this single story changed the perception of Samaritans. Today, hospitals and relief organizations choose to identify with the Samaritan, even though they are historically neither Jewish nor Christian. Even in popular language, when anyone offers assistance to a stranger, we refer to the helper as "a good Samaritan."

The day Jesus told the story, however, surrounded by Jewish people trained for centuries to distrust and dislike Samaritans, this parable took, in their minds, a strange turn. The Samaritan stranger did everything the religious leaders should have done and more. He felt compassion, personally bandaged the injured man's wounds, placed the man on the Samaritan's animal, took him to a public inn for care, and handled all the expenses (vv. 33-35).

We can only imagine what every person present was thinking. It is virtually certain they were all stunned and emotionally involved in the story, perhaps each wondering how this unusual tale answered the question: "Who is my neighbor?"

The Surprising Ending (vv. 36-37)

The lawyer had planned to ask Jesus questions He couldn't answer. Instead, Jesus asked the lawyer a question that ended the debate. Jesus asked, "Which of these three, do you think, proved to be a neighbor to the man who fell among the robbers?" (v. 36). Of course the biblical scholar was left defenseless; there is clearly only one answer. The Jewish scholar still could not bring himself to say the word *Samaritan*. Instead, he tried one last, weak, unsuccessful evasive ploy. He acknowledged "the one who showed him mercy" was the real "neighbor" to the injured man (v. 37). Then Jesus turned the conversation in an unexpected direction when He replied, "You go, and do likewise."

The original question was, "Who is my neighbor?" The implication is, "Who is qualified to be my neighbor?" Inherent in the question is the unspoken, "Whom can I avoid? Who is not qualified to be my neighbor? Which person or group of people does not deserve my mercy?"

Remember, this conversation began with both the lawyer and Jesus agreeing that each of us should love our neighbor as we love ourselves (vv. 27-29). Who then is included? Jesus reversed the thinking of the question by making clear the neighbor is not someone near you. You are the neighbor. Your actions, not the other person's, determine who your neighbor is and whom you are to love.

The world changed a little when Jesus told that story. The simple tale of the merciful Samaritan, the natural enemy, reminds us that mercy recognizes no ethnicity and allows no excuses when people need our help. For two thousand years the parable of the good Samaritan has challenged us to love and help without discrimination.

The humanity of one person helping another quieted the critic's invective. It still can. Luke included this parable to make certain we are left with no doubt about what Jesus would do. And now we know what we should do too.

For Memory and Meditation

"Which of these three, do you think, proved to be a neighbor to the man who fell among the robbers?" He said, "The one who showed him mercy." And Jesus said to him, "You go, and do likewise." (Luke 10:36-37)

---

[1] Elizabeth Chuck, "Fact Sheet: Who Has Nuclear Weapons, and How Many Do They Have?" NBC News, March 31, 2016, https://www .nbcnews.com/news/world/fact-sheet-who-has-nuclear-weapons-how -many-do-they-n548481.

Chapter 5

One Thing

Luke 10:38-42

How distracted are we? We know it's an issue, but are we just now admitting how serious the issue has become? The current guilty culprit, as we all know, is technology. For instance, recent research shows average smartphone users check their phone on average about eighty-five times a day. When a research team put an app on study participants' phones to track use, the average time spent online, checking messages, or using apps was about five hours a day—roughly one-third of our waking hours every day![1]

Few would deny the advantages of a smartphone (I'm writing this chapter on mine right now), but the easy availability to information, entertainment, and social media through our phones has a downside too; we are living distracted lives.

A recent *New York Times* article addressed the issue of technology distraction. The article cited information from a new book analyzing the ways technology affects our brains. The authors concluded that when we are online "we willingly accept the loss of concentration and focus, the division of our attention and fragmentation of our thoughts."[2] As any employer, parent, teacher, or highway patrolman will tell you, a distracted person is a less effective person.

We know distractions affect our work, jeopardize our safety while driving, and frustrate those around us when we don't pay attention, but what are the implications of distractions on our spiritual lives? One of the events in Jesus's life, found only in the Gospel of Luke, speaks directly to the issue of spiritual distractions.

Friends of Jesus (vv. 38-39)

Barely two miles from Jerusalem on the descending eastern slope of the Mount of Olives in today's West Bank is the village of Bethany where friends of Jesus lived. Martha, Mary, and their brother Lazarus are the subject of several significant New Testament stories spread across all four Gospels but mentioned directly by name only in Luke and John. The stories about the little family of siblings offer us unique insights into both the public ministry and the less public life of Jesus as He interacted with them in their home. In addition, the frequency in which Jesus stayed in Bethany, in instances where the three are not directly identified, implies even more interaction with His three friends.

In those passages where they are mentioned, we are able to draw a consistent composite portrait of their temperaments, as well as their lifestyles. By comparing multiple passages we get a glimpse into what appears to be the life of a wealthy family. In Luke's Gospel they live in a house sufficiently large to accommodate the Lord and His apostles. The group numbered at least thirteen men and perhaps a few others who often traveled with Jesus and His disciples (Matt. 27:55; Mark 15:40-41; Luke 8:1-3).

Another example of their probable financial situation is found in John's Gospel and implied in Matthew and Mark.

John informs us Jesus was invited to what appears to be a banquet in His honor in Bethany where Martha was the hostess and oversaw the details of the meal (John 12:1-2). This same story is told in Matthew and Mark, but in those Gospels neither Martha nor Mary is mentioned by name. Instead, the dinner party in Bethany, in the days before the crucifixion, was hosted in a home known as the house of Simon the Leper.

Imagining a leper hosting a dinner party is impossible, so perhaps the name of the house was still associated with a man who had previously owned the house and had since moved on or died. In any event the time (just prior to the crucifixion), the occasion (a dinner in honor of Jesus), the place (Bethany), and an unexpected dispute (the potential waste of a perfume) make clear that the dinner where Martha was hostess is the same party held in Simon the Leper's house. Nothing is said about the relationship between Martha and Simon, but Simon may have been the deceased father of the three well-known siblings who had inherited the house after their father's death. The banquet, in any case, is another example of the family hosting a large gathering and apparently covering the expenses.

Finally, the wealth of the three friends of Jesus is perhaps most obvious by the use of an expensive perfume Mary poured on Jesus (John 12:1-5). A bottle of perfume worth almost a year's salary is not likely to be found in the residence of a poor family. These three were affluent for their time, and with their wealth and privilege they often ministered to Jesus and His followers.

Another interesting detail about these three is that, unlike almost everyone else frequently mentioned and associated with Jesus in the Gospels, these three are never seen following Jesus from place to place. They did not give up their house as other disciples did. Instead, every reference in the Gospels concerning Martha, Mary, and Lazarus mentions them at their house in Bethany. They didn't go with Jesus as He traveled; He came to them when He wanted to rest.

The Personalities (vv. 38-39)

Martha is appropriately named since her name is the feminine version of the Greek word translated into English as *master*. The house where Jesus went for dinner in verse 38 is referred to as Martha's house, even though she had a sister and a brother living there. When a banquet was given for Jesus in Matthew's, Mark's, and John's Gospels, Martha is the hostess, clearly in charge of the details. Martha is in charge everywhere we meet her.

Martha's sister, Mary, on the other hand, is portrayed in Scripture with a different temperament. In the three passages where we see Mary, she is always at Jesus's feet. First, we are told in verse 39 she "sat at the Lord's feet." Next, in the story of the raising of Lazarus when Jesus arrived at their house, Mary "fell at His feet" (John 11:32). Finally, at the anointing of Jesus in Bethany with the expensive perfume, Mary wiped Jesus's feet with her hair. Again, she was at His feet (John 12:3).

These temperamental differences between the two sisters serve as the basis for the dispute that arose when Jesus and His disciples were eating at the sisters' house (Luke 10:40). Martha was busy serving and attending to details, and Mary was sitting. It was a recipe for trouble.

Distractions (vv. 38-42)

Jesus must have had a personal relationship with Martha, Mary, and Lazarus that differed from the relationships He enjoyed with most of the other people He encountered. For one thing Jesus is always seen at their house rather than meeting them in passing or traveling with them. In addition, their relationship appears less formal in some ways than with other people who may not have known Him as well. For instance, the centurion in Capernaum couldn't conceive of Jesus's even entering his house (Matt. 8:5-10). The woman with the constant blood flow merely wanted to touch the fringe of His garments instead of speaking to Him (Matt. 9:20-22). Many other people Jesus healed were met only in passing as He traveled through the villages of Galilee. The relationship He had with Martha, Mary, and Lazarus is more akin to a close, personal friendship.

Martha's demanding tone when addressing Jesus also suggests her familiarity in His presence. When she was serving the dinner for Jesus and His team of followers, she grew agitated with Mary for leaving her to handle the details, and she appears stern and intolerant in her opinion of Jesus for encouraging Mary's inactivity.

The scene is easy to imagine. Martha was originally happy Jesus and His followers had come to her home. Luke says she "welcomed" Him and the group to her house. The Greek verb translated "welcomed" is used only a few times in the New Testament. It is first used here and is used all but once by Luke. It always signifies a joyous, hospitable reception of guests into a home.

The focus of Luke's Gospel is deliberately on Jesus, so

the disciples play a less significant role than in the other Gospels. In fact, if one is familiar with the four Gospels, a comparative reading of Luke's Gospel reveals a detached and overt lack of concern with the apostles' activities. When they are mentioned, it is frequently in a less than positive light. Luke will, however, turn his literary attention toward the disciples when he pens Acts. So, while the immediate action of Luke's narrative about the meal surrounds only Jesus, Martha, and Mary, we should assume the entire group arrived at Martha's house because Luke says, "They went" (10:38).

The presence of the entire group helps explain why Martha was so exasperated with her sister. If the only people present that day were the two sisters and Jesus, it's hard to see how such a small meal could be so disruptive to a take-charge, organized leader like Martha. However, if the entire band of disciples were there, as they surely were, then the meal was for at least fifteen people. Preparing, serving, and cleaning up a dinner party of that size would feel overwhelming to one person. Martha was busy with every detail of the meal but couldn't help noticing her sister Mary sitting, apparently ignoring all the work. Martha's type-A personality was reaching a boiling point! Ironically, she blamed Jesus rather than Mary and aimed her frustration at her guest rather than her roommate. Martha insisted, in a noticeably harsh and demanding tone, that Jesus do something about her sister's casual negligence, by implicating Jesus as being uncaring (v. 40). It was a strange moment.

Why did Martha react as she did? Why did she temporarily seem to forget whom she was entertaining that day? Luke tells us. Martha was "distracted" (v. 40). This word occurs only here in the Greek New Testament and is beautiful in its descriptive power. Made up of two common Greek words, it creates an uncommonly clear picture of Martha's mental state. It comes from the Greek word usually translated as "around" and is the verb from which we get our English word *spasm*. The word paints a vivid picture of Martha's frenetic activity. She was "spinning in circles" with concern about dishes, pots, and pans; and in the process she had lost all focus concerning what was most important.

As Martha fumed around the house, Jesus responded by assessing the source of Martha's agitation. Jesus addressed Martha by saying her name twice. This repetition of a name or title is common in Luke's writings. In Luke 22:31, for instance, Jesus warned Simon Peter of the temptations and spiritual warfare he would face. Jesus addressed him by saying, "Simon, Simon." The same repetition of a name was used in Acts 9:4 on the road to Damascus when Jesus famously addressed Saul of Tarsus as "Saul, Saul." Luke's writings contain numerous other instances of repetition of names or titles, and all of them seem to be used to get the attention of the one addressed or to stress the importance of the message being communicated. When Jesus addresses individuals with the dual mention of their name, however, an additional purpose appears to be involved. In addition to getting the person's attention, Jesus seems to be appealing to the person's sense of reason. He is reasoning with Martha. Hearing her name repeated was a way to calm her so she could listen.

According to Jesus, Martha was "anxious" (Luke

10:41). The Greek root word used to describe Martha's anxiety means "to divide" or "separate into parts." The idea couldn't be more obvious. Martha's anxiety was an expression of a divided attention and a lack of focus. She had too many things on her mind. Jesus also diagnosed her as "troubled," a word from which we derive our English word *disturbed* or *turbulent*. In other words, her thoughts were chaotic and disheveled. Whenever we see Martha in the New Testament, she is outwardly organized and handling multiple details at once, but in this story we get a glimpse into her inner life. Inwardly she was anxious and feeling out of control. Why did the normally controlled and controlling Martha feel so chaotic and frenzied? Jesus said she was "anxious and troubled about many things" (v. 41). The focus on "many things" that day led to her being out of focus. Jesus was in her house. Jesus was teaching around her kitchen table, and she was obsessing about skillets, spoons, and dirty dishes!

We are Martha. Instead of a first-century woman in the Middle East, Martha looks like a twenty-first-century believer trying to multitask through our obsessive interests in the things around us. Meanwhile, we sometimes seem barely mindful of the presence of the Lord near us. When we allow ourselves to become spiritually distracted, several problems develop. For one thing, we lose focus, forget what matters most, and pay too much attention to matters of secondary importance. We can also easily become agitated, angry, and accusatory toward the people around us when all the while the problem is within us. Martha's intentions about service and excellence were commendable, but her spiritual life was a mess!

Devotion (vv. 41-42)

Mary, in contrast to Martha, says nothing in this passage. Instead, she has chosen a quiet disciple's path in relationship to Jesus. She is sitting at Jesus's feet, a symbol of submission. She is representative of a disciple who has recognized and responded to the lordship of Christ. In fact, the word *Lord* occurs three times in this brief narrative. Luke observed that Mary "sat at the Lord's feet" (v. 39). Martha then ironically challenges the decision-making judgment of Jesus by addressing Him with the incongruent statement, "Lord, do you not care . . . ?" (v. 40). Luke then tells us, "But the Lord answered her" (v. 41). One contemporary New Testament scholar suggests a fourth example of lordship in this passage is woven into the picture of Mary's sitting at the feet of Jesus. He makes an astute and informed observation regarding the fourfold focus on Jesus as Lord in such a brief story. "Even for Luke, who regularly introduces this title in his narration, this is extraordinary."[3]

It is always helpful to step back from any biblical text and ask a challenging question: "Why did the author include this passage?" We believe the text is inspired by the Spirit of God, and we also believe the Spirit chose Luke, with all of his personal insights and skills, to write under the inspiration of the Spirit by bringing all of himself to the task. Luke selected numerous events from the life of Jesus that occur nowhere else in the New Testament, and it helps us understand the passages if we know why Luke added what he did. One of Luke's purposes for wedging this short story into his long narrative appears to be to demonstrate that Jesus is Lord of all and deserves our attention and undistracted surrender to His lordship.

Mary chose to surrender and submit to His lordship, demonstrated by the fact she "listened to His teaching" (v. 39). Jesus commended Mary by contrasting her to Martha. Martha was busy and anxious about "many things," but Mary had wisely chosen "one thing" (vv. 41-42). In fact, Jesus insisted the decision to pay attention to His teaching is the priority in the Christian life that is "necessary." The word *necessary* suggests the duty of the disciple's life is more important than the urgent tasks associated with daily living. Learning from Him and His teaching is the "one thing" every disciple must do if we want to follow Him as Lord, even if some of the other demands of life go unanswered. This lesson is hard for distracted disciples to learn, living the way we do in the mad rush of the twenty-first century.

The real question posed by this story is not about our willingness to focus on the disciplined management of our few years in this life. Martha's failure is not found in the fact she wanted to live well by attending to the important as well as the mundane tasks of life, including cleaning up dirty dishes after a meal. We should applaud her for her determination and willingness to serve. The real question is: Will we allow the numerous demands of this brief life to hold first place while we neglect the Word of the Lord, even though it is so accessible?

Are you a distracted disciple? Have you temporarily lost sight of the "one thing" that is most important? This little, unique slice of life when two sisters welcomed Jesus into their home questions our priorities in life and begs the question regarding what or who is "Lord" over us. The good news is that Jesus says we have a choice. Jesus said, "Mary has chosen the good portion." If Mary could choose, so can you. If she could identify the "one thing" most necessary in life, so can you.

Luke ends the little snapshot of Jewish home life with a promise for every distracted disciple. The promise is from Jesus. If you choose the "one thing" over the "many things," it "will not be taken away" (v. 42). You must choose between distraction and devotion. Which will it be?

For Memory and Meditation

"But the Lord answered her, 'Martha, Martha, you are anxious and troubled about many things, but one thing is necessary. Mary has chosen the good portion, which will not be taken away from her.'" (Luke 10:41-42)

---

[1]Victoria Woollaston, "How Often Do You Check Your Phone?" *Daily Mail*, October 29, 2015, http://www.dailymail.co.uk/sciencetech /article-3294994/How-check-phone-Average-user-picks-device-85 -times-DAY-twice-realise.html.

[2]Tony Schwartz, "Addicted to Distraction," *The New York Times*, November 28, 2015, https://www.nytimes.com/2015/11/29/opinion /sunday/addicted-to-distraction.html.

[3]Joel B. Green, *The Gospel of Luke,* The New International Commentary on the New Testament (Grand Rapids, MI: Wm. B. Eerdmans, 1997), 434.

Chapter 6

Father and Son

Luke 15:11-32

On a beautiful, sunny autumn morning I drove a good distance to attend a prayer meeting. But the only prayer I remember from that meeting was a father's painful prayer for a missing son. After brief instructions from the meeting's leader, about thirty men knelt at cushioned pews throughout the little worship center. A man I didn't know started praying for his son. The story he told us after the prayer was terrible. Years had passed since he had seen his son. The young man and the father had argued about everything. The father, earlier in his life, had criticized his son's long hair and lifestyle, and one morning the argument got intense. The son stormed out of the house and let the screen door slam hard behind him as he thundered out of the driveway. Days turned into decades, but the father never saw his son again. So he prayed and waited, just as he had done every day for years. The son was gone, vanished without a trace; and it looked as if he would never return.

I don't think I will ever forget that man's tears or the story he told of his remorse over letting his son leave. None of us that day knew what had happened to the son, but all of us could see what had happened to the father. His heart had been ripped out, and every day was an empty, dull reminder of what might have been. My son was about three years old at the time, and I could scarcely imagine anything worse than wondering for a lifetime if you would ever see your child again.

Maybe it's the innate sense inside all of us, the universal knowledge that the love of our family is one of the most meaningful aspects of our lives, that makes the story Jesus told about a father and a son so remarkable. Only Luke recounts the parable of the prodigal son, but it may be the most famous story Jesus ever told.

Parables about Lost Things (vv. 1-32)

Luke records three of Jesus's parables that clearly fit together. The first involves a lost sheep, the second is about a lost coin, and the third is the story of a lost son. The lost sheep was one of one hundred. The lost coin was one of ten. The lost son was one of two. With each story the stakes got higher. There is nothing greater than recovering a lost person.

In each parable the moral of the story is the same: when that which was lost is found, there is a reason to rejoice. In the first two parables Jesus sums up the story with the conclusion that just as we rejoice when something valuable is found, so there is rejoicing in heaven when lost people repent. In the final parable, however, Jesus lets the characters in the story do all the explaining. In a sense the other parables, which are excellent little parables about the urgency of searching for the lost, are merely preparatory for the story of the lost and recovered son.

Consider this: in the first two parables Luke uses only five verses each. The story of the prodigal son, however, while using an economy of words to communicate so much, nevertheless uses twenty-two verses to tell the story of the recovered son. The parables about lost things reach their summit in the parable about the lost son.

One difference of interest in the three stories is subtle yet noticeable. In the first two parables the lost things are recovered because the people who lost them search for them until they are found. In the story of the father and his sons, however, the father allows the younger son to leave and only runs to the son when he is within sight of being home, having returned because he realized being away from the father was foolish.

The father did not wait passively, however, for the son to walk all the way back home before rushing to greet and welcome him. The point is made in a slightly different way in the parable of the lost son, but in all three stories God clearly searches for the lost and eagerly welcomes the sinner who comes to God.

In the end the parables all demonstrate God's interest in recovering lost sinners who are far from Him because He cares about them. The entire chapter is actually one long answer to a complaint about the relationship of Jesus to sinners lodged by "the Pharisees and the scribes" (v. 2). The Pharisees were leaders of the local synagogues and represented less than 5 percent of the Jewish population, yet their importance to the community was much greater than their number. Scribes were likewise teachers of the Old Testament law who studied the Scripture and taught disciples of their own. The scribes were often Pharisees themselves (Mark 2:16).

The two groups of religious leaders were constantly accusing Jesus of wrongdoing and eventually led the way in calling for and plotting His execution (Luke 19:47). In Luke 15 they grumbled against Jesus because they said He "receives sinners and eats with them" (v. 2). We can find an abundance of literature explaining the rationale behind the religious leaders' objection to eating with "sinners." They must have extrapolated that view from passages like those found in Psalm 1:1, which reminds godly people not to walk "in the counsel of the wicked" or stand "in the way of sinners" or sit "in the seat of scoffers."

From a Christian perspective we might interpret those admonitions as calls to personal holiness and to not allow ourselves to emulate the lifestyle of evil people. The religious leaders in question, however, were not so much concerned with whether they would be influenced by evil people. Instead, they were concerned about ceremonial cleansing, and therefore they often classified people as "sinners" because most people were unable to maintain the strict ceremonial purity needed to worship regularly in the temple. No wonder Jesus called out the religious leaders for their hypocrisy. To the very group so apparently concerned with eating with "sinners," Jesus said, "Woe to you, scribes and Pharisees, hypocrites! For you are like whitewashed tombs, which outwardly appear beautiful, but within are full of dead people's bones and all uncleanness" (Matt. 23:27).

But even if we took the most generous view toward the religious leaders and gave them the benefit of the doubt regarding their own motives for not eating with "sinners," what was their issue with Jesus's doing it? If they considered Jesus a "sinner," why did they concern themselves with His eating habits?

Jesus was right about them. They were "dead" spiritually, and everything about Jesus exposed them as "whitewashed tombs." They were so clueless about God's real love for lost people that they failed to see that their criticism of Jesus, that He associated with sinners, was in fact the reason so many people rallied to Him then and still do today. He did not come to "call the righteous but sinners to repentance" (Luke 5:32).

The three parables about rejoicing when lost sinners are found were all direct answers to the Pharisees and scribes' bizarre criticism. Little did they realize that Jesus came to do more than eat with sinners. He came to call them to repentance and faith so they could live, which thrills the heart of God! All three parables tell that story.

The Parable of the Lost Son (vv. 11-32)

Have you ever noticed how few words Jesus needed to tell a story in a way that sums up the characters, the tension, and the plot? Within three brief verses we are introduced to a family and presented with a problem that needed to be solved. Two thousand years later we still regard the story of the prodigal son as one of the most effective short stories ever written. Beyond its literary value, we learn a truth about God's mercy that has given people hope since the first day the story was told.

The Youngest Son (vv. 11-16)

A man has two sons, and the youngest son felt impatient about an inheritance. Subtly we determine the man is affluent since poor families in Jewish culture would be focused on making enough each day to survive. The younger son knows a lot of money is coming his way when his father dies. The fact he requested the inheritance immediately carries a note of selfish cruelty. It was as if he was saying, "I can't wait for you to die. I want it now." The Old Testament prescribed the amount of the inheritance. The older son received two-thirds of the father's wealth, and the younger son would be entitled to the rest (Deut. 21:17). As Jesus is telling the story, we are struck with the audacity of the request; but the story, for the time being, ignores another detail. There is an older son, and he will be affected by this request, too. His story comes later, and his role is a significant part of Jesus's larger message.

Generally parables are told to communicate one point, and the various details of the story exist to serve the major point. Everything else should be considered incidental and not relevant to the story's main subject. Why the son was able to convince his father to go along with this ill-advised scheme is not an important piece of the story. In fact, it is a necessary detail that the father allows it, thus creating the dilemma that eventually leads the young man home. In other words, trying to evaluate every detail of a parable to learn a lesson about God's nature or His kingdom becomes an exercise beyond the purpose Jesus intended and probably leads us away from the main point.

Within a short time after the request is granted, the younger son has converted property to cash assets and leaves for a distant country. We are not explicitly told the family was Jewish, but it is almost certain the first hearers would have naturally assumed it and would have had no reason to consider anything else. The place he went is not important, other than the fact the young man left the

Jewish land of promise to live alone among Gentiles. Jesus is telling this story in such a way that the average Jewish listener would naturally form a poor opinion of the young man and his choices.

Jesus reaches the turning point in the story quickly. The young man was reckless and foolish with his money. Jesus said the younger son "squandered" his money in "reckless living" (v. 13). This young man is living a life few could respect. The Greek word translated "squandered" comes from a word used to describe the process of winnowing grain. The agricultural communities of Israel understood the process. Grain was piled up, and a winnowing fork, a cross between a pitchfork and a rake, was used to lift the grain and toss it in the air. The breeze blew the lighter, inedible, worthless chaff away while the heavier, edible grain fell back to the ground. That's how the younger son lost one-third of his father's wealth and all of his inheritance. He blew it! His lifestyle was reckless, a word with a spiritual connotation. It could be translated "unsaved." It is the same word Paul used to describe the result of a drunken lifestyle, "excess" (Eph. 5:18 KJV). The younger son is the epitome of the old expression, "A fool and his money are soon parted." The story is already a moral tale and a tragedy, and the young man looks, at the least, ungrateful, irresponsible, and selfish. Jesus has used barely over sixty English words to arrive at this point in the story. But it gets worse!

Jesus is painting a picture of a lost son in vivid colors. After the son's bad judgment led to losing everything he had, the worst-case scenario occurred. A famine in the land destroyed the economy of the country. That meant others were in need, and others were no doubt out of work from the "severe famine" (Luke 15:14-15). People who spoke the language and had local connections were probably looking for work, and with an economy in recession, the jobs were scarce. The young man from a foreign country couldn't find any meaningful work, and the situation was quickly going from bad to worse!

If it seems things couldn't worsen, Jesus finds a way to take the young man down even lower. He started working at a pig farm. Working with pigs had to be the worst situation imaginable for a young Jewish man. It couldn't possibly get any more regrettable, but it did. The younger son started looking at the pigs' food, and it looked good! He had hit rock bottom.

My Father (vv. 17-21)

The young man has a change of heart while in the pigpen. He starts to remember the benefits of life on the family farm. He reflects on the goodness of his father who treated even his hired hands better than the son was living now. Why wouldn't he simply go home? He could start over and work with the other employees in his father's massive operation. They were eating generous helpings of good food while the young man was considering the cuisine of hogs as a viable option. His resolve rings with determination: "I will arise and go to my father" (v. 18). Ultimately this resolve is the turning point Jesus wants for sinners: the Father is the solution.

He started walking, and with each step he was rehearsing a prepared speech to show his repentance and remorse over what he had previously done. He left home with assumptions about what was owed to him as a son. He was returning with no misgivings. He did not feel worthy to be called a son. He was in for a surprise.

Jesus reintroduces the father at this point. The son is dragging himself back home with low expectations, but the father is watching the road. In the distance he sees a familiar figure. The father's love for his son filled him with compassion. The broken young man coming up the road was decidedly different. The clothes of privilege are now rags, filthy from his long journey and his time in the hog lot. His confident swagger is gone. Pride has been replaced with a sense of being wrong about everything he once believed about himself and his father. He had sinned, and he knew it.

The father could not contain his joy and started running to meet the son who had returned. As they met, the father wrapped his arms around the young son and kissed him. He called his employees to come and celebrate with him. The father was ready to restore the privileges of sonship on the returning son. A new robe, shoes, the family ring—all signs of being welcomed back to the family—were readily offered. He ordered that a special calf being fattened for a special occasion be prepared for the night. The entire household would be invited. The lost son had been found. It was time to celebrate.

The father's reaction reiterates the conclusion of the first two parables. When a sinner repents, there is rejoicing in heaven (vv. 7, 10). Jesus described the rejoicing of heaven in common terms we understand. Family, friends, good food, upbeat music from a live band, and celebratory dancing were on the agenda. It was an idyllic scene except for one loose thread. Earlier in the story Jesus had mentioned another son, an older brother, and his reintroduction into the story puts a damper on the festivities.

The Other Son (vv. 25-32)

The older brother's role in the parable of the prodigal son complicates the structure of the story, making the plot more complex, but gives us an additional glimpse into the merciful heart of the father. The older brother is angry when he learns the irresponsible younger brother had come back. He is introduced as being "in the field" (v. 25). Once again the brilliance of Jesus's storytelling genius is on full display. The younger son was brash and irresponsible, but the older son is hard at work. We might expect him to be heroic, but he's got problems too. He is jealous of the party and makes derogatory and inflammatory comments about his little brother, accusing him of spending his money on "prostitutes." He complains the fattened calf has been sacrificed while he never had even "a young goat" at a party with his friends (vv. 29-30). His responses are both realistic and, at the same time, almost comical in their childishness.

The father once again comes to one of his sons. The father in this parable takes initiative and wants to reconcile the sons to himself, regardless of why they feel unwelcome in their father's home. The younger son felt unworthy and had to be reassured. The older son feels neglected and entitled, and the father assures him he shares in the inheritance if only he will recognize the joy of recovering one who was "dead, and is alive; . . . was lost, and is found" (v. 32).

The story ends with the conflict unresolved. The only

thing certain is the father's joy when a son is restored. The Pharisees and scribes who had criticized Jesus for eating with sinners should have felt a pang of conviction when Jesus introduced the dutiful older brother who refused to eat with his sinful little brother. It seems most likely Jesus fashioned the older brother in the likeness of the self-righteous Pharisees. The one thing certain in the abrupt conclusion is the father's joy when a son is restored. Jesus accomplished two things with this parable: He answered his critics for the moment and reaffirmed His mission to "seek and to save the lost" (19:10).

For Memory and Meditation

"For the Son of Man came to seek and to save the lost." (Luke 19:10)

Chapter 7

Speaking of Hell

Luke 16:19-31

Jesus told a story about a poor guy who went to heaven and a rich guy who went to hell. No one else in the New Testament records this story. Why does Luke? More importantly, what does Jesus want us to learn from the long, graphic parable of the rich man and Lazarus?

Overview

The story of the rich man and the beggar named Lazarus begins with an introduction of the wealthy man and a synopsis of the vast extent of his wealth. Jesus then introduces Lazarus and explains in vivid detail how destitute he was in the days before he died.

After a brief introduction of the two men, they both die. The rich man wakes up in hell and sees the poor man Lazarus in the distance, comforted in the eternal presence of Abraham, the Father of the Faithful. The rich man wants out of hell but learns that is not an option. He wants some relief from the torture and finds that, too, is out of the question. At last he wants someone to warn his wealthy family so they won't go to hell, but he is told they have access to the truth already. Even a miracle won't save them if they ignore the warnings they already have but choose to ignore.

Like the parable of the prodigal son, the parable of the rich man and Lazarus has a complex plotline with long, involved conversations. What is the main point?

Luke is consistent throughout his Gospel in his portrayal of Jesus and His special identification with and care for the poor. The Gospel writer also records strong warnings to the rich. For instance, when Mary learns she is expecting the Messiah, she praises the Lord because "he has filled the hungry with good things, and the rich he has sent away empty" (1:53). Later, the ethical preaching of John the Baptist sounds a note of social justice when the crowds ask him what is required of them to show their repentance. He instructs them to give their extra coat to the person with no coat. The tax collectors are told to refrain from taxing the people more than is required. Finally, soldiers are taught to stop using extortion to get money from innocent people and to learn to be content with their wages. These practical instructions from John the Baptist intentionally stress money, possessions, and greed (3:10-14).

While the list of Luke's concerns about poverty, wealth, and greed could grow unusually long, one other example should be noted. Jesus declared in His hometown address that He had been anointed by the Spirit "to proclaim good news to the poor" (4:18).

It isn't that the other Gospels do not address these same concerns, because they do. The difference is Luke drives home the principles time and time again in some of the most breathtaking and convincing arguments and story lines found in the New Testament. In addition, he places his concern for the poor on the lips of unassailable messengers like the virgin Mary, John the Baptist, and, most convincingly, Jesus of Nazareth. After all, only Luke revealed the birthplace of the King of kings was a cattle stall (2:7). Luke is building a case, demonstrating God's love for the poor. After a while, the stack of evidence gets too deep to ignore. Luke repeatedly presses his argument concerning God's mercy toward the poor.

To properly understand the parable of the rich man and Lazarus, the consistent themes of wealth and poverty must be kept in view. In addition, since the most compelling drama in the parable takes place in the afterlife, we can't limit the discussions about the meaning of the parable to some economic or political system we may imagine Luke wants to establish. This parable begins in the lap of luxury and ends in hell. That cannot be ignored.

Context (vv. 1-13)

The parable of the rich man and Lazarus is told from the vantage point of a larger context. The chapter opens with a pointed discussion about wealth management in the form of another parable. Like the parables of the prodigal son and the rich man and Lazarus, the first parable in Luke 16 is unique to Luke with only the concluding verse (v. 13) bearing a similarity to a portion of the Sermon on the Mount in Matthew (Matt. 6:24).

The parable of the dishonest manager—or the unjust steward, as it is traditionally known—is hard to understand because it is complicated by levels of duplicity, schemes, and half-truths. It is difficult, therefore, to determine who the hero is and what Kingdom principle we are to learn from it. For our purposes here it is enough to recognize Luke is using economic principles to teach the lessons about the Kingdom. For one thing, how we handle money is a test of character used to determine our readiness for spiritual blessings (vv. 10-12). Second, we are reminded by Luke what we learned also in Matthew: we cannot serve both God and money (v. 13; Matt. 6:24).

After Jesus told the parable of the dishonest manager, the Pharisees reacted. They found the idea of comparing our personal wealth to our spiritual lives ludicrous (v. 14). They ridiculed Jesus for His comparison. Luke explained their reaction by confiding an open secret; the Pharisees "were lovers of money" (v. 14). In spite of their ridicule (a word that literally means they "turned their noses up"), Jesus warned them they were justified only in their own minds. Their greed, however, was unhidden from God's scrutiny, and He judged it to be "an abomination" (v. 15). After this episode with the Pharisees and their mockery, Jesus doubled down on His warnings about the relationship between how we manage wealth and our eternal souls.

Jesus responded to their derision by telling the parable of the rich man and Lazarus. The story of a wealthy Jew going to hell while an indigent beggar entered heaven couldn't be regarded as a laughing matter to anyone who believes in a coming judgment.

After We Die (vv. 19-31)

In early 2018 a false alarm for an incoming ballistic missile headed toward Hawaii warned people to seek immediate shelter. The scene of tourists and residents scrambling for safety was one of panic and confusion. People were huddling in the safest places they could find, clinging to their families, and fearing the worst: a nuclear strike from North

Korea. One fifty-six-year-old tourist from Los Angeles, California was in a hotel room and started crying immediately, knowing a nuclear ballistic missile meant the end.[1]

Can you imagine waiting for a missile armed with a nuclear warhead to hit your city? Those terrified people were in one of the most beautiful places on earth. Many of them were on vacation, but instead of enjoying their vacation, they all thought they were going to die.

Most of us don't think about death much. We know it will occur, but we don't want to dwell on it. Most people don't dwell much on what happens after they die either. But Jesus knew exactly what happens, so one day He told us.

Some may object and suggest the parable about the rich man and Lazarus is only a parable, a story and not an actual event. True, it is a parable, but all of Jesus's parables emerge out of real-life experiences and believable scenarios about oil lamps, weddings, crooked politicians, godly widows, and planting crops. A parable uses one true thing we can understand to help us comprehend another true thing that is more difficult to understand. The story about the afterlife in the parable of the rich man and Lazarus is the ultimate example of clarifying truth. Jesus never used a falsehood to prove a truth. Had He done so, it would have made the truth He was illustrating suspect.

Additionally, if this clear explanation of what happens after we die is not true, then Jesus has confused His point rather than clarified it. If, in fact, the places described are not real, then we are left with a simple question: What does this parable mean? Ultimately, if that were the case, I believe it would mean nothing at all.

Luke can sum up a man's life in a few words. He tells us the rich man wore the expensive, purple clothes of royalty and gorged on rich foods the average Israelite could only dream about. Every day was a feast fit for a king. At this rich man's gate was a beggar near death. The beggar was starving and covered with open wounds. He was so weak he couldn't lift his arms to wave away packs of dogs licking his bloody wounds. Had he received only scraps of food from the rich man's daily banquets, he might have lived a little longer, but it never happened. He died in the street—sick, hungry, and alone.

These two men could not be more different. The rich man had it all, and Lazarus had nothing except a name. Actually, Lazarus is the only person in all of Jesus's parables who is given a name. It was the only thing he had when he died that day outside the rich man's luxury mansion, surrounded by those wild dogs.

As different as they were, the two men did have one thing in common: death. It happens to the rich and the poor. Death is the great equalizer. But, just as they were different in life, they were also different after death. The tables had turned. One man was in heaven. The other man was in hell.

Luke described Lazarus as being "carried by the angels to Abraham's side" (v. 22). That description of what happened to Lazarus is full of hope and comfort. He died alone, but after death God sent angelic pallbearers to lift him out of the street and into the presence of one of the greatest men in Jewish history. Abraham was God's friend and the father of all the faithful. What reward could a Jewish beggar dying in the streets hope for after death?

Certainly occupying the same proximity to the Father of the Faithful would not have seemed possible. Before his death Lazarus was a nobody. He didn't even have a friend to protect him from animals roaming the streets. But after death Lazarus was with Abraham. It was heaven.

In the instant after death, the rich man awoke in horror. He was in hades (v. 23). He was in instant torment and anguish due to the burning fire of hell. He could see Abraham in the distance. He saw Lazarus. The nameless rich man started crying because of the flames. He was begging for even a drop of water. Maybe Lazarus could help him, the man he suddenly remembered as being the same one who used to lie outside his outer gate. The rich man knew the poor man's name after all; it was Lazarus. Yet, in spite of knowing him and being aware of his plight in life, the rich man never threw Lazarus even a crumb from the daily feasts. Everything, however, looked different from hell.

The rich man begged for mercy in the form of a drop of water. But the answer was no. Yet even in final rejection tenderness existed from the other side. Abraham addressed the rich man as "child" or "son" (v. 25 NIV). Clearly the rich man was from the chosen race. The words that came next are frightening. Abraham said, "Remember" (v. 25).

What is hell like? Those in hell have sensations of thirst and pain. They can see. They can speak. They can hear. They recognize themselves, and they recognize others. But what may be the most terrible reality of hell is the ability to "remember." Remember all those times you ignored Lazarus. Remember how many times you could have done things differently. Hell is an eternity of regret.

Abraham explained the situation. In life the two men

were on the opposite ends of the economic spectrum. In eternity they are also in different places. Lazarus was in comfort now. The rich man was in anguish now. The situations had been reversed but also amplified beyond description. Life was short. Eternity is long. In life things might have been different. In the afterlife there is no chance of change.

Abraham added the solemn note of finality when he drew the rich man's attention to a chasm between heaven and hell. No one crosses that canyon. There is no escape and no relief. It is forever.

The story Jesus told presents us with a horrifying picture. Since most of us want to avoid thinking about death, the fact of an eternal place of conscious torment is almost unimaginable. Yet Jesus affirms without equivocation there is life after death, including a place of reward and a place of punishment. Hell is the worst place imaginable. It must be avoided. No one should want to go to hell. So the most important and urgent question is: How can anyone keep from going there? Is it merely as simple as rich people go to hell, and poor people go to heaven?

The message of Luke teaches God's loving concern for the poor and condemns greed, but nowhere in Luke's Gospel, or anywhere else in the New Testament, is our eternal destiny determined by our financial status at the time of our death.

Two related questions emerge at this point. The first question is twofold: Why did Jesus tell this story, and why did Luke include it? Second, since the parable revolves around our eternal destiny, does it answer the question of how we avoid hell?

In His inaugural message in Nazareth, Jesus promised to "proclaim good news to the poor" and "the year of the Lord's favor" (4:18-19). So, by relating the parable, both Jesus and Luke advanced Jesus's agenda, which included offering the good news to even the poorest of the poor and simultaneously proclaiming salvation had come.

As to whether the parable explains how to avoid hell, the answer is twofold. First, no parable is a complete explanation of the way of salvation. That isn't their purpose. Instead, the parables illustrate aspects of Jesus's kingdom message. This parable demonstrates that what matters in eternity and the values of Jesus are not the same as the common standards used by most people to determine their values.

The Pharisees ridiculed the idea that their greed and love of money could impact their eternal destiny. This parable strikes at the heart of that view. Luke wants us to see that being a wealthy Jewish man is of no greater value on God's scales of judgment than if you are a beggar lying in the street. God's judgment about where we spend eternity will not be based on either our packed portfolios or our poverty. Both are irrelevant in eternity. So how does one avoid hell?

An Invitation from Hell (vv. 27-31)

At this point the parable could have ended and served as a powerful cautionary tale. But as is typical of some of Jesus's parables in Luke, the plot took a twist. There was more to the story.

When the rich man realized all hope for him was gone, his thoughts turned to his family. He didn't want them to join him in hades. So he became an intercessor. He appealed from hell for the resurrection of Lazarus so he could go back from the grave and warn the rich man's five brothers who, he felt certain, were as doomed as he was. Unfortunately, the answer was again no. The rich man was learning that after you arrive at your eternal destiny, it's too late to rethink what should have been. Still, there was hope for the five greedy, wealthy brothers.

Abraham explained it to the rich man, "They have Moses and the Prophets; let them hear them" (v. 29). At this point the rich man argued but revealed a previously unspoken truth. He knew he had lived an unrepentant life. His real problem had not been money. His problem, he acknowledges, had been sin.

Ironically he had not learned his lesson because he still argued with heaven about the terms of receiving life. When Abraham said the brothers had the answer in "Moses and the Prophets," the man in hell said, "No, father Abraham, but if someone goes to them from the dead, they will repent" (v. 30).

At that point Abraham says something astonishing. "He said to him, 'If they do not hear Moses and the Prophets, neither will they be convinced if someone should rise from the dead'" (v. 31). We know the gospel of Jesus Christ was good news because Jesus has been raised from the dead. Therefore, even the resurrection of Jesus would not convince those who had the Bible but refused to believe it.

The story of the man in hell ends there, but Luke leaves his readers something to consider, which would become clear later. In two separate resurrection appearances of Jesus, the Lord would make plain to his disciples that His entire ministry had been predicted in the Law of Moses, the Prophets, and the Psalms (24:27, 44). Jesus taught the Old Testament message pointed to His life, death, and resurrection. In other words, the parable of the rich man and Lazarus concludes with an invitation. Luke is making a strong argument that the message of Jesus was found in the Old Testament. Trusting Jesus, therefore, is the only way to heaven and the only way to avoid hell.

For Memory and Meditation

"No servant can serve two masters, for either he will hate the one and love the other, or he will be devoted to the one and despise the other." (Luke 16:13)

---

[1]Jolyn Rosa, "Tears and Panic as False Missile Alert Unnerves Hawaii," Reuters, January 13, 2018, https://www.reuters.com/article /us-usa-missiles-falsealarm-people/tears-and-panic-as-false-missile -alert-unnerves-hawaii-idUSKBN1F300K.

Chapter 8

The Jericho Man

Luke 19:1-10

Have you ever said too much and realized you were in way over your head? Or maybe you know what it's like to anger the people around you, even though you thought you had a great idea. An old friend of mine has a saying for times like that: "Why don't you quit while you're behind?"

From the earliest days of His ministry, Jesus said and did things that polarized people. His hometown tried to kill Him after one of His sermons, and religious leaders plotted His death from nearly the beginning of His ministry. If Jesus had been running for a political office, perhaps He would have conducted polls and surveys or focus groups to refine His message. Maybe that way He could have stayed out of so much trouble. Fortunately, Jesus wasn't running for anything. He didn't need to refine His message. He knew exactly why He had come. He meant what He said, He knew His purpose, and He stayed on message and on task. Unfortunately, religious leaders were His most visible and persistent opponents.

Given what we know about Jesus today, why did anyone object to Jesus's teachings or His actions? Frequently the issue that kept Jesus at odds with religious leaders had to do with the company He kept. He loved to associate with sinners! Some people never get comfortable with that.

Jesus and Sinners

Throughout the book of Luke, Jesus is consistently associated with a group of people the religious leaders of His day called "sinners." As a result, the leaders took a dim view of Jesus's ministry. Of course, the negative perspective of His opponents eventually escalated to His death on the cross. In the most basic analysis, the ultimate problem, which led to the crucifixion, started with the difference of opinions about sinners.

Almost immediately after Jesus started calling His disciples, the criticism from the religious leaders began. From the religious leaders' perspective, tax collectors were certainly in the category of "sinners." After all, they collected taxes from their fellow Jews, but the income from those taxes went to the despised Roman government. When Jesus called Levi the tax collector (also named Matthew, the author of the Gospel by that name), Levi was so overjoyed with grace that he invited all his notorious friends from the tax collectors' network to his house for a meal and to meet Jesus. Most of us would see that as a "win" and exactly how evangelism and the kingdom of God should work. The religious leaders, however, were not interested in evangelism. Instead, they were interested in protecting their narrow interests, which they publicly, officially, and erroneously maintained were actually God's interests. It was a complicated and perverted misinterpretation of the Old Testament, which Jesus never supported and consistently opposed from the beginning of His ministry. Therefore, when the infamous tax collectors gathered at Levi/Matthew's home for a meal with Jesus, the Pharisees raised an objection. Luke tells us, "And the Pharisees and their scribes grumbled at his disciples, saying, 'Why do you eat and drink with tax collectors and sinners?'" (5:30). Jesus clarified the issue. He wasn't spending time with the "sinners" to commend their sin. His purpose was redemption. "And Jesus answered them, 'Those who are well have no need of a physician, but those who are sick. I have not come to call the righteous but sinners to repentance'" (5:31-32). While Jesus's response is crystal clear and easily understood, the Pharisees apparently rejected it. The problem would continue.

Sometime later, in an unrelated context, Jesus responded again to the criticism, which apparently was gaining momentum since He refers to the charge as if it were a commonly held allegation. Jesus said, "For John the Baptist has come eating no bread and drinking no wine, and you say, 'He has a demon.' The Son of Man has come eating and drinking, and you say, 'Look at him! A glutton and a drunkard, a friend of tax collectors and sinners!'" (7:33-34).

Numerous other examples of the clash over the relationship with "sinners" could be cited from Luke's Gospel. One additional instance, however, perhaps best demonstrates the prevalence of the misunderstanding.

Jesus was invited by a Pharisee to a dinner at the Pharisee's house. In an odd, spontaneous moment, a woman from the city with a reputation for some undisclosed sin came in and started anointing the feet of Jesus, kissing

His feet, and wiping them with her hair. The religious leader was stunned. He thought to himself, "If this man were a prophet, he would have known who and what sort of woman this is who is touching him, for she is a sinner" (7:39).

Jesus attracted people who were guilty of all kinds of well-known sins. His willingness to eat with them, minister to them, and genuinely care for them put Him at odds with the religious establishment from the beginning of His public life.

After two thousand years, sometimes even the most well-meaning Christians still haven't grasped the concept of accepting and loving people. In one congregation I was happy to serve, I led a lady I met during our "street ministry" to Christ. She was unconventional by almost any standard. I met her husband too. They had a place to stay, but it was unclean and in a dangerous area where drugs and crime were common. I had been in places like that before, but this was about the worst. They were part of the indigent poor of that community, but when they came to Christ, it was a happy day in their difficult lives.

I baptized both of them, and they started attending church regularly. They were a sweet couple with a lot of needs. The staff members all knew them by name, and we all loved them. They were happy to be following Christ and attending church. But the inevitable happened.

One Sunday an immaculately dressed lady from the congregation approached me about the woman from the street. She spoke to me so politely in that large, well-decorated room where they met for Sunday School. She informed me the other ladies were concerned, and she shared their concerns about the street lady who had started attending their Sunday School class. The ladies felt their class wasn't a good fit for this new member. She probably couldn't be happy in their class, could she? There had to be a different class somewhere where she would be happier.

The church lady that day was kind and nice to me, but I knew what she was saying. The street lady with the benevolence-room wig didn't fit the profile of the wealthy widows who attended that class. It was true. She was from the street! She couldn't hide that.

As the reality of what I was hearing sunk in, I felt a hollow sense of defeat, mixed simultaneously with a closely guarded anger. I realized the woman from the street would never be welcomed into that group. Maybe I should have known that before I introduced her into the class. But I was young, and I was learning. It was part of my unofficial education into ministry. We shouldn't be surprised about the cultural prejudice Jesus battled every day. We still have similar battles, don't we?

In His culture Jesus deliberately pushed the boundaries of accepted norms. And invariably we still push against our culture when we follow His call to go into the real world to win lost people.

In spite of His critics, Jesus went out of His way to earn the title "friend of sinners." That constant theme in Jesus's life and Luke's Gospel leads us to an encounter with a man in Jericho, in a tree.

Zacchaeus (vv. 1-7)

We're accustomed to aerial photos and satellite images, but in the first century climbing a tree was a good option if one wanted a better view. One of Jesus's last overt outreaches to a man, publicly identified as a "sinner," occurred in the city of Jericho. The first time Jesus saw him, Zacchaeus was in a tree.

Humor, of course, is a subjective art. Still, the scene of Jesus's calling a potential disciple out of a tree looks like an example of Luke's expert use of language and the art of telling a story. The entire scene is woven together to subtly create a lightly humorous moment. Even the description and cadence of the action is Lukan narrative at its artistic best: Zacchaeus "climbed up" before Jesus "looked up." Jesus said "come down," and Zacchaeus "came down" (vv. 4-6).

The weight of the Lukan narrative's subject matter will not provide the reader with an opportunity for an emotional break after this story. By the time Jesus passes through Jericho, He is nearing Jerusalem for the last time. He is traveling toward the cross. Ultimately, the motive behind this unusual story is the loving mercy of Jesus's seeking another sinner before time runs out.

Everything about the account of Jesus's ministry as He was passing through Jericho is included in Luke's Gospel to highlight Jesus's special love for the outcast, the disadvantaged, and the poor. For instance, as He "drew near" to Jericho, He healed a blind beggar, even though the blind man was discouraged by the crowd from seeking Jesus's help (18:35-39). Then, as He entered Jericho, Jesus encountered a man on the other end of the economic scale who was rich but whose career was frequently included with the most despised members of society. The Pharisees regularly "grumbled" that Jesus chose to eat with "tax collectors and sinners" (5:30). Jesus was aware of the critics' vitriol and even once quoted them when they lumped the "tax collectors and sinners" together (7:34). Finally, Luke observed that "tax collectors and sinners were all drawing near" to Jesus (15:1). Zacchaeus was a tax collector.

As Jesus came into Jericho, traveling southwest on His way to Jerusalem, He had attracted an entourage of nameless people, eager to surround Jesus the "miracle worker." Yet, in spite of the eager crowd presumably filled with human need, Jesus spotted a diminutive man in a tree looking down and turned His attention solely on him. Luke gives us a rare physical description of the man (the New Testament offers painfully few physical descriptions) and tells us he was short. Therefore, he needed to climb the tree for practical reasons. He couldn't see Jesus since most of the people in the crowd were taller than he was.

What Jesus said to the short tax collector in the tree demonstrates, in powerful theological overtones, God's far-reaching purposes in grace. Jesus called Zacchaeus by name and said, "I must stay at your house" (19:5). Jesus did not say, "I want to come to your house." He said, "I must." Jesus was under a divine mandate. He picked one man out of an entire city. The man was a tax collector, too—the kind of person that kept Jesus in perpetual dispute with the religious leaders. The religious leaders must have assumed Jesus just wouldn't learn His lesson. That must be a partial reason Luke records the conversation in the crowd with predictable language: "They all grumbled, 'He has gone in to be the guest of a man who is a sinner'" (v. 7).

What they didn't know, however, is that every time Jesus ministered to a poor outcast or a sinful woman or a tax collector, He wasn't the one needing to learn a lesson. He was teaching all of us a lesson if we are ready to learn it. Zacchaeus, the tax collector, isn't an unusual outlier in the divine plan. He is Exhibit A in what Jesus had set out to do from the beginning: seek sinners!

Exuberant Repentance (vv. 8-9)

The transition from the tree on the side of the busy street to the tax collector's house is almost undetectable in the English text. Yet Luke uses a word that describes welcoming guests into the home (v. 6). The crowd refers to Jesus's leaving to be his guest (v. 7). Zacchaeus abruptly stands up, though we weren't told he had been seated (v. 8). Finally, Jesus declares that "salvation has come to this house" (v. 9).

It is clear from these words and phrases that Jesus had gone to the man's home. Jesus, therefore, is doing again what had kept negative conversation about Him current and unrelenting throughout His ministry. He associated with "tax collectors and sinners." Obviously, Jesus fully intended to continue ministering to the outcast and the disregarded until the end of His life on earth, and Luke fully intended to highlight that deliberate feature of Jesus's life.

The interesting fact about the encounter between Jesus and Zacchaeus is the excited response of the tax collector. He stood to speak. We must draw some conclusions from silence since Luke doesn't include many details we might wish were included. Can we reasonably assume they were reclining at a table for a meal? Perhaps that is a reasonable assumption, though it must remain only speculative in the absence of any detailed explanation. Were the disciples present? Again, it seems probable given the context. Jesus and His troupe were traveling to Jerusalem together, and we might naturally conclude, with some confidence, they stayed together when Jesus went to the tax collector's house. So let's reconstruct the scene by supplying the most probable missing pieces.

The likely scenario must have unfolded something like this: Jesus and all His disciples went to the tax collector's home where they all enjoyed a meal. During the meal Jesus talked with Zacchaeus about the kingdom of God. The tax collector reached a conclusion, and Luke finishes the story. The tax collector jumped to his feet with an announcement: He had decided to give half of his assets to assist the poor. In addition, "if" he had "defrauded anyone" he would pay back "fourfold." In other words, if he took one dollar, he would repay with four dollars. That is a 300 percent interest rate!

Jesus summarized, "Salvation has come to this house" (v. 9). We shouldn't conclude that altruistic giving of huge sums of money to worthy causes is the way to be saved. Instead, Jesus is pointing out the obvious: Zacchaeus was a changed man.

Luke doesn't tell us if Zacchaeus was overcome with tears or if his repentance was accompanied by a sense of grief over his past sins. We don't see him in sackcloth and ashes. Instead, we get the picture of a man jumping up to declare how different he feels about himself and the world around him. He is boisterous and declarative. He seems happy! He acts like a man released from jail! Jesus had set the prisoner free (4:18).

The citizens of Jericho "grumbled" about Jesus's interest in the dishonest tax collector. The religious authorities would never understand. But to the broken and the sinful people who received the focus of Jesus's mercy, He was the best Friend a sinner ever had. Even Christians sometimes forget how being lost feels.

Years ago I was privileged to serve two wonderful churches in the Atlanta area during the years while Ted Turner was still in charge of his broadcasting empire. One day the news reported that the billionaire had publicly announced, unceremoniously, Christianity is "a religion for losers."[1] You can imagine the outrage in the Christian community. People were disgusted and angry. How dare he refer to us as "losers"! Yet when I heard it, I wasn't offended. I had seen Jesus minister to "losers" many times. I had friends who had "lost" the battle with addictions. I knew men who had "lost" their families. I had personally ministered to people who had "lost" their personal freedoms and were serving time in prison for the crimes they had committed. In fact, I knew of many of my own sins that would have landed me on a list with "tax collectors and sinners" had I lived in first-century Jerusalem. So, after all of the "losers" I had seen helped by Jesus, I wasn't offended in the least by the mogul's insult.

When I had a chance to address my congregation the next Sunday after the news broke, I said, "Thank God Jesus is for losers, because it's certain almost no one else is for them. I thank God Jesus is for every loser I've ever known, including me!"

Seek and Save (v. 10)

The final verse in the story about Zacchaeus sums up not only the event in Jericho but in a larger way also serves as a summary for the book of Luke. Beyond that, the verse accurately sums up the entire ministry of Jesus, the Christian message, and the only hope a sinner will ever find. Jesus said, "For the Son of Man came to seek and to save the lost" (v. 10).

The religious culture of judgment may never understand or appreciate the depths of that pronouncement. Some others may casually accept it as a form of religious entitlement, as if Jesus owes us what He went through to save us. Still, many others ignore the words of Jesus completely. But for those who have ever looked at their own lives with honest discernment and recognized flaws that run deep into the fabric of their souls, they get it. For those who have stumbled repeatedly over the same self-defeating obstacles along the path of life or have hurt the ones closest to them because of fixations and obsessions they couldn't control, they often are the first to recognize they need the help Jesus offers. For those whose guilty past looms larger in their minds than their discredited future, they know they need Jesus to seek and save them because they've learned He is the only one who will.

It often seems the disregarded and the spiritually broken tend to respond most readily to the good news that Jesus is seeking them. They are often desperate to believe He is for them, even if they have been aggressively against Him in the past.

If you are anything like me or anything like the Jericho

man, the best news you've ever heard is that Jesus seeks and saves sinners.

For Memory and Meditation

"For the Son of Man came to seek and to save the lost." (Luke 19:10)

---

[1]Ann O'Neill, "The reinvention of Ted Turner," CNN, November 17, 2013, http://www.cnn.com/2013/11/17/us/ted-turner-profile/index .html.

Chapter 9

Jesus on Trial

Luke 23:6-16

Even as a child I was fascinated with religious artwork. The oversized family Bibles my parents and grandparents had on their coffee tables were full of the glossy prints of famous paintings from the past. One of my favorites was the depiction of the Last Supper by the fifteenth-century Italian artist, Leonardo da Vinci. I studied the figures in the painting and wondered why they were reacting as they do. I have admired the painting for as long as I can remember.

When I visited Italy a few years ago, along with the expected trips to see the Vatican, feed the pigeons, ride the gondolas in Venice, and photograph the Leaning Tower of Pisa, I made sure we went to Milan to see da Vinci's original masterpiece, *The Last Supper*. I wasn't prepared for what I saw!

It is massive for one thing. It is painted on a wall inside a church. Time has certainly damaged the work, but viewing it is an almost overwhelming emotional experience. One American lady standing near me wept as she looked at it. I think I had tears in my eyes as well.

What would you think of me if while standing in front of one of history's greatest works of art I began to criticize the colors chosen by the artist or the facial expressions of the apostles? Would you think I was out of my depth? You would be correct. What if you interrupted my harangue to inform me *The Last Supper* is one of the well-loved masterpieces in the world, only for me to casually shoot back, "Well, I took an art class in college, and I just don't see what all the fuss is about." You might be tempted to call for security to escort me out while serious people viewed the artwork.

The fact is that most of us are not in a position to critique the world-famous painting. It has earned a place in the hearts of millions and is beyond our judgment.

If that is true for great works of art, how much more mind-boggling is it that one night in Jerusalem a Roman governor with little appreciation for Old Testament prophecies, along with a weak local despot with a guilty conscience, conspired with a group of petty but devious religious leaders to judge Jesus Christ? As bizarre as it seems, it happened, and as a result, the greatest miscarriage of justice transpired while unwittingly fulfilling ancient biblical prophecy.

All four Gospels conclude with the arrest, trial, crucifixion, and resurrection of Jesus. Familiar details include Jesus's prayer and arrest in the garden of Gethsemane, the chaotic "trial" before the ruling elders of Judaism, the composure of Jesus when He appeared before Pontus Pilate, and, eventually, His death on the cross. Each account includes minor unique features. For instance, Mark mentions a young man fleeing naked from the arrest scene. In another example, Matthew goes into slightly more detail following the man's ear being cut off by one of the disciples while attempting to protect Jesus during the arrest. Only

John, however, actually identifies Simon Peter as the one who injured the man. The Synoptics only refer to the fact "one of them" used the sword. In any case these are the kinds of small details that differ. The crucifixion story itself provides us with additional, minor facts, and all are understandable additions from the perspectives of the individual writers who for their own purposes added local color.

When it comes to the trial, however, Luke gives us a major detail never addressed by the other Gospels. His perspective about the trial of Jesus is unparalleled.

The Night of Betrayal (22:14–23:16)

It's difficult to say for certain how long Jesus was in the upper room for the Passover meal on the last night of His life. We know it was an evening meal that began after sundown in the spring of the year when the days are getting longer. There are several essential components in the Passover meal, along with cultural variations. Today, for instance, it isn't unheard of for a Jewish family to enjoy the traditional Passover meal until past midnight.[1]

While we can't be certain how long Jesus and His disciples lingered over that last Passover meal, it is difficult to imagine any of them attempting to rush through it. Why would they? In addition to the meal itself, Jesus washed the disciples' feet and gave us some of the richest teaching about discipleship found in the New Testament. All the additional teaching occurred in the upper room after the meal (John 13–17). It is reasonable to assume we have only the summary of the incredible teaching shared that night. The same is true of His "High Priestly Prayer," which also took place after His final Passover (John 17).

I am dwelling on all this to help us establish a rough estimate of the timeline for the events of that night. From nightfall until the time Jesus and His disciples started walking toward the garden of Gethsemane, several hours had passed. By the time they got to the garden, it was deep into the night. Once they arrived, Jesus appears to have spent up to three hours in prayer before the arrest occurred. It was at least well past midnight. Jesus and His disciples had to have been exhausted, but the long night was just beginning.

As Jesus was concluding His Gethsemane prayer, the silence of the night was interrupted by the sound of a group marching aggressively into the garden. The large crowd was an odd assortment of chief priests, officers of the temple, Roman soldiers, and Judas, a disciple of Jesus leading the way to betray Jesus.

The Trials (23:1-16)

All the Gospels record the fact Jesus was forcibly escorted out of the garden and led back across the Kidron Valley, up the hill to the house of Caiaphas, the high priest. Modern visitors to the Holy Land are routinely taken to a place called The Church of Saint Peter in Gallicantu, which is historically believed to be where Caiaphas's house stood. Alongside that building are the ruins of ancient stone steps, reported to be from the time of Christ. If these locations are accurate, one can easily envision the fairly brief and direct route taken from Gethsemane to the place of the first trial, in front of a group of Jewish leaders called the Sanhedrin (Matt. 26:59).

After the hectic and emotion-driven trial in front of the

Jewish elders, Jesus was taken to the Roman governor Pontius Pilate. Pilate is mentioned in all four Gospels and Acts and is presented as a conflicted character. He clearly did not want to execute Jesus. Perhaps his reluctance is best represented by his symbolic gesture of washing his hands in front of the crowd, telling them he was "innocent" of the death of Jesus (Matt. 27:24). While he may have wanted to declare himself innocent, he was far from it.

Earlier in Luke's Gospel we are told, in a passing description of Pilate's bloodthirsty approach to leadership, that when a group of Galileans had gone to the temple to offer sacrifices, Pilate had them executed and added their blood to their sacrifice (13:1). To think that the high priest who is responsible for the temple and its ceremonial purity would conspire with a man who so treacherously desecrated the temple by allowing Jewish blood to be offered on the altar is almost inconceivable. It is a reminder of how corrupt the priests had become and how desperately they wanted Jesus eliminated.

When the Jewish leaders questioned Jesus in Luke 22:66-67, they wanted to know only one thing: Did He claim to be the Christ and the Son of God? When they took Him to Pilate, however, their accusations weren't based on religious concerns about alleged blasphemy. Instead, they presented Jesus to Pilate with political charges. They said Jesus aspired to be a king in competition with Caesar, and He was challenging the Jewish people to stop paying taxes to Rome (23:2).

Obviously the charges were untrue, but Pilate perked up when he heard the word *king*. He inquired if Jesus considered Himself to be a king (v. 3). Jesus answered with an understated affirmation. Pilate, however, quickly lost interest, seeing nothing in Jesus that posed a threat to Rome's international power base.

Pilate confirmed what Luke's readers already knew: Jesus was innocent of the charges leveled against Him. Pilate found "no guilt" in Jesus (v. 4).

The Jews were frantic, however, and alluded to Jesus's Galilean roots (v. 5). Pilate sensed a way out of what he obviously considered unnecessary drama so early in the morning. He pounced on the Galilean connection and hurriedly sent Jesus to Herod. At this point Luke's unparalleled Gospel presents us with a brief encounter between Jesus and Herod not found in the other three Gospels.

Who Is Herod? (vv. 6-16)

Even for those familiar with the New Testament, the numerous leaders with the name Herod can get confusing. We are familiar with Herod the Great who reigned over Israel when John the Baptist and Jesus were born (1:5). That Herod was the duplicitous tyrant who had hoped to murder Jesus as an infant. When he could not locate the whereabouts of the baby Jesus, he ordered the brutal and heartless execution of every male toddler under the age of two years in the town of Bethlehem (Matt. 2:1-18). He died while Jesus was an infant, but he had reigned for decades before.

Herod's skill as a builder is still evident today with numerous, impressive ruins bearing evidence of his architectural ambitions. Perhaps one of the most obvious remains of his massive building projects is Masada, which Herod built as a palace in the Judean desert. Other major building projects included his multiyear project of renovating the temple at Jerusalem (including the Western Wall, one of the most frequented places in modern Jerusalem). Herod also developed the city and the seaport in beautiful Caesarea Maritima. While the harbor has been destroyed, the amphitheater he built there is still used today.

Following Herod the Great, his sons ruled portions of Israel. Herod Archelaus and Herod Phillip I are less well known to New Testament readers than their brother Herod Antipas. Antipas is presented in the New Testament as a weak-willed ruler who allowed himself to be manipulated by his wife (whom he had seduced away from his brother, Herod Phillip I) into executing John the Baptist. Even though Herod was personally fascinated by John and had developed a somewhat personal relationship with him, when the time came, at the insistence of his wife, Herod ordered the decapitation of John the Baptist (Mark 6:17-28).

Originally, when Herod Antipas heard about the ministry of Jesus, he superstitiously assumed Jesus was working miracles because He was the resurrection of John the Baptist (Matt. 14:1-2). Herod's conscience bothered him but never enough to lead him to change. This Herod, a man lacking the courage of character, would eventually sit in judgment over Jesus.

The other Herods in the New Testament include a father and a son who are both named Agrippa. Herod Agrippa I was the grandson of Herod the Great and had the apostle James executed (Acts 12:2). Later, his son, Herod Agrippa II, became the ruler who entered into an incestuous and scandalous relationship with his sister, Bernice. These two heard Paul the apostle's defense at Caesarea Maritima (Acts 25:23–26:32).

The Herod who had John the Baptist killed also played a role in the trial of Jesus. He proved to be shortsighted and cruel and, like many others in power, unable to recognize a real King.

The Trial under Herod (vv. 6-12)

After assuming Jesus was a miracle worker because He was a phantasm or the spirit of John the Baptist, Herod was eager to meet Jesus when Pilate sent the Lord to him on that early spring morning. His interest in Jesus was superficial and in no way implies an interest on his part to join the Christian family. Instead, Herod's interest in Jesus had to do with a curiosity about miracles. One might naturally assume a ruler who controlled a miracle worker might gain more prestige and power for himself. Jesus, however, would not oblige Herod's occultist misunderstanding of Jesus's power. As a result, the meeting between Herod and Jesus was relatively brief.

Herod enjoyed seeing Jesus. In fact, the persistent oddity about Herod was his unusual interest in godly men. They were so unlike him. Herod drank too much, was disloyal, and made no effort to disguise his lusts and sexual appetites. He was morally bankrupt, and it left him fearful and easily manipulated. Yet when John the Baptist, one of the most spiritually disciplined and morally upright people in history, spoke, Herod was all ears. Still, when the time came, in order to save face, Herod ordered the execution of John the Baptist. The only thing that could be trusted about Herod Antipas, it appears, is he could always be trusted to take care of his own life and interests first.

The opportunity to meet Jesus was at least as intriguing to Herod as questioning John the Baptist had been. When word came in the early hours on Friday that Pilate was sending Jesus to Herod, whatever he had planned that morning became secondary. Herod wanted to see miracles. He hurriedly agreed to see Jesus. It ended as the greatest missed opportunity in Herod's selfish life.

Herod peppered Jesus with questions as Jesus stood before him on trial. The Jewish religious leaders simultaneously stood by, making one slanderous accusation against Jesus after another. In the midst of the scene, we see Jesus silently enduring it all. Herod could get no information from Jesus, and Jesus refused to use His celebrated miraculous power.

In a parting gesture of abuse, Herod allowed the soldiers to do what they wanted with Jesus, which included mockery and contemptuous treatment. They even dressed Jesus in expensive robes as a form of ridicule, before sending Him back to Pilate. Herod thought the whole thing was a joke, and He treated the incident as some form of personal entertainment until he grew bored and sent Jesus away. For Herod, the whole thing was anticlimactic and a meaningless waste of time.

Herod is a dichotomy. He knew John was a prophet of God, and yet he had him killed. He thought Jesus was the resurrection from the dead of the prophet John the Baptist with the power to work miracles. Yet he dismissed Jesus and mocked Him as He left.

In some ways Herod was a man like many others. He

was given multiple opportunities to hear and understand the message of the gospel, but he refused to believe it or act on it. He merely dismissed the Lord and ridiculed what he couldn't understand. It is difficult to see Herod as much more than a petty, pleasure-seeking, hollow man who, when given the opportunity to meet Jesus, failed to grasp the importance of the moment. He foolishly laughed away his one meeting with Jesus as if it had been nothing more than another vacuous attempt to find entertainment to feed his boredom.

Herod is a reminder that seeing isn't always believing, since he had personal contact with both John the Baptist and Jesus and missed the opportunity to repent and believe both times! Luke successfully wedged the nearly forgotten story of Jesus before Herod into the timeline for the trials of Jesus in order to demonstrate, yet again, there was no guilt in Jesus. That morning in Jerusalem Herod had the power to put Jesus on trial, but history has exonerated Jesus and found Herod and his self-aggrandizing contemporaries guilty of looking at life and choosing death.

In a much less historic way, whenever we think about the claims of Jesus for our lives and try to decide whether we will refuse them or obey them, we put Jesus on trial in our own way. We act as if it is solely in our power to decide if we will follow Jesus's teachings. We easily forget that the same teachings we put on trial put us on trial. We close our eyes to the fact Jesus is watching for our obedience while we're weighing His commands.

On the day Herod met Jesus, the world thought Jesus was on trial before Herod. In hindsight, we see it was the other way around.

For Memory and Meditation

"Then said Pilate to the chief priests and to the people, I find no fault in this man." (Luke 23:4 KJV)

---

[1] "Ask the Expert: New Seder," My Jewish Learning, accessed February 2, 2018, https://www.myjewishlearning.com/article/ask-the-expert-new-seder/.

Chapter 10

The Last Words of Jesus of Nazareth

Luke 23:28-46

Jesus is nailed to the cross. He doesn't have long to live. His mission is nearing completion. In those agonizing moments we will hear the last words of Jesus.

The outcome of the trials of Jesus was never in question. For his part Pilate, the Roman governor of Judea, navigated the choppy waters of high emotion, attempting to avoid crucifying an innocent man. In the end it was impossible to quiet or satiate the relatively small group of religious leaders who continued to vociferously demand Jesus's death. There was no due process. Instead, there was a rush to judgment and execution. In fact, the first trial before Pilate occurred extremely early Friday morning (John 19:14). Jesus was dismissed to be tried by Herod and returned for a second "trial" before Pilate. The Roman governor brought Jesus before a crowd and offered to free Jesus or another prisoner named Barabbas. The assembled crowd shouted for the death of Jesus by crucifixion.

After the public had their say in the matter, Pilate sent Jesus to be savagely beaten by the process known as flogging (John 19:1). It left Jesus weak and bloody. Luke never mentions the action other than to imply it would happen (Luke 23:16).

The place where Jesus was crucified had an ominous name, Golgotha or "The Skull" (v. 33). It was probably the common place used by the Romans for crucifixions. Hence it developed the moniker "The Skull" as a way of describing it as a place of death. The second option for the unusual name may be because the place resembled a human skull. The location's name has remained an important part of the story of Jesus's death. The Greek word for skull is *kranion*, from which we derive our English word *cranium*. The King James Version uses the Latin word for skull, *Calvariae*, in Luke's Gospel, so the place is often referred to as "Calvary." Finally, the Aramaic word for "skull" is *Golgotha*, which is mentioned by the other three Gospels (Matt. 27:33; Mark 15:22; John 19:17). The name *Golgotha* is almost as popular in the common Christian vocabulary as *Calvary*. The four Gospels agree the place where Jesus was crucified was "The Skull." Even though we frequently call it by different names, they all mean the same thing.

In recent years the brutality of the crucifixion has become a standard part of preaching and teaching, especially in the evangelical branch of the Christian family tree. Artwork and movies have also become more graphic in portraying the death of Jesus. Yet the Gospels all approach His death in a much more understated manner. For instance, blood is not mentioned in any of the Gospel accounts of the crucifixion, except when John mentions the mixture of blood and water that poured out when the soldier pierced Jesus's side (John 19:34).

None of the Gospels mention nails in the crucifixion

account, either. They are mentioned indirectly when the skeptical disciple Thomas blurts out his refusal to believe in the resurrection unless he sees in the resurrected Jesus the "mark of the nails" in His hands (John 20:25). The Gospel writers were less interested in describing the graphic details of how Jesus died and more focused on the fact that He died and that His death on the cross had always been central to the plan of Jesus (Luke 24:44-46).

Perhaps an additional reason the Gospels did not describe the horrors of the cross had to do with the fact people in the ancient world knew about crucifixion from personal experiences. There were many crucifixions. Everyone had seen them. They knew grown men were stripped for humiliation and then nailed to the cross. How can civilized people today even comprehend this barbarian form of capital punishment? Unfortunately, due to the scourge of global terrorism, we are hearing of crucifixions again.

In spite of the fact that crucifixions are not part of our normal experience as they were for first-century Jews, except in infrequent news reports of isolated actions in distant places, we do have an English word that reminds us of the cross. We have a term for pain that reaches a ten on the pain scale ending in ten. Ten-out-of-ten pain is unbearable. We call that kind of pain "excruciating." It's the worst kind of suffering. The English language looks back two thousand years to find the appropriate way to describe indescribable pain. Excruciating pain is literally pain "out from the cross."

In the first century the process of crucifixion was repeated often in capital punishment cases. The cross was laid on the ground so the victim could be nailed firmly to the heavy, wooden beam. Then, with the criminal suffering an agony impossible to imagine, the cross was raised up and dropped into a deep hole so it could stand upright. When the cross reached the bottom of the hole, the weight of the man violently forced him down while the nails held him to the cross. In that vulnerable, terrible moment, he must have felt every nerve in his body light up like he had been set on fire. There really is no way to imagine the torture human beings had to endure on the cross.

Once the cross was upright, the man would begin to die a slow, terrible, public death. There is not a single historical record of anyone surviving crucifixion. It was the end. Crosses were hung in busy places on well-traveled roads as a deterrent to future crimes. The Romans wanted people to know what kind of "justice" they could expect if they were found guilty of misdeeds.

Because their hands were nailed high and their bodies dragged down by gravity, a crucified man's immediate dilemma was finding the least painful way to breathe. Because of their physical position on the cross, breathing was labored; and as time passed, their weakness made pulling up to exhale and inhale again increasingly difficult. It was a slow, inhuman way to die. That's how Jesus of Nazareth died.

The Last Words (vv. 32-46)

Beginning as early as AD 170, Tatian, a Syrian disciple of Justin Martyr, attempted the first known "harmony" of the Gospels. In his harmony the final words of Jesus were grouped together for teaching and study.[1]

Jesus died quickly during the six hours He was on the cross, but He uttered seven brief statements. Three of them are exclusive to John. Three are only found in Luke, and one other is repeated in both Matthew and Mark. The seven sayings are: "Father, forgive them, for they know not what they do" (v. 34). "Truly, I say to you, today you will be with me in paradise" (v. 43). "Woman, behold, your son. . . . Behold, your mother!" (John 19:26-27). "My God, my God, why have you forsaken me?" (Matt. 27:46; Mark 15:34). "I thirst" (John 19:28). "It is finished" (John 19:30). "Father, into your hands I commit my spirit!" (Luke 23:46).

From this list we find three unparalleled statements from the cross unique to Luke's Gospel. The first, second, and final statements from the cross are all found only in Luke. Let's examine them more closely.

"Forgive Them" (vv. 32-34)

I have two daughters. One works in advertising; the other works in public relations. They amaze me with their understanding of how the public responds to and processes information. Having listened to them discuss their respective industries, I doubt they would attempt to present a client or a product to the world using the client's most humiliating moments as the lead story. But as a writer, Luke does just that and goes to extraordinary lengths, as do all of the Gospels, to show Christ's humiliation at the cross. For instance, we are familiar with the seven sayings from the cross, but another interesting study is of the sayings to the cross! In other words, Jesus was not merely speaking to the air. Multiple dialogues and conversations were taking place between Jesus and others throughout the day. The mockery was part of the humiliation for the condemned man.

One of the subtle mockeries taking place, which Luke uses to tell his story, is the fact Jesus was crucified as a criminal between two other criminals! As if the suffering of the cross was not enough, the indignity of dying in a public crucifixion with criminals is a crucial part of understanding why Luke included the sayings he did. Luke wants to demonstrate that Jesus not only suffered physically on the cross, but He also bore every shame and indignity possible on our behalf, and none of it was deserved! Jesus willingly "endured the cross, despising the shame" (Heb. 12:2).

When Jesus arrived at The Skull, He was joined by two other men, both described as "criminals" (Luke 23:32). The Greek word translated "criminals," is made up of a combination of two Greek words literally translated "evil workers" or "wrongdoers." The word is used only four times in the Greek New Testament, and three of those instances are in Luke's telling of the crucifixion and are all within eight verses (vv. 32-39)! Luke is deliberately drawing our attention to the scene of the Son of God dying among criminals guilty of capital crimes.

Luke also revealed insights into Jesus's mind-set during the crucifixion. Had He given up hope? Did He feel defeated? Was He afraid? The first saying from the cross clarifies to what degree the Lord was still on mission, even as He died on the cross.

As Jesus was raised up on the cross, He said, "Forgive them" (v. 34). What have you ever done that possibly compares with the guilt of the soldiers and others who physically nailed Jesus to the cross? It is not immediately clear whom Jesus is referring to when He asks for His tormentors to be forgiven. Did He mean to include the Sanhedrin? Was He referring to those who stood by the cross and mocked Him? Did He mean every person who ever lived? The immediate context suggests, at the very least, all those responsible for His death, especially those who were standing close enough to hear Him speak, must be included as the guilty parties for whom He interceded.

If He was willing to forgive them, what does that say about Jesus of Nazareth and His willingness to deal with and forgive sin? For Him to go voluntarily to the cross, He had to go willing to pay the penalty of sin. If He would die for sinners, surely He would pray for them! If we ever feel a need for mercy and are drawn to grace, Jesus is the Savior we seek. His first words from the cross clarify forever the kind of Messiah He is. He is an intercessor and a substitute for the undeserving, and He desires the forgiveness of the guiltiest among us, even before we have given any thought to our need.

"You Will Be with Me" (vv. 39-43)

The theme of the mockery of Jesus continued beyond the implied humiliation of dying between criminals, when the criminals themselves started mocking Him! "The humiliation and repudiation of Jesus are underscored in many ways in this co-text, but none more dishonoring than His being spurned by a criminal, by one whose place in mainstream society had already been categorically dismissed."[2]

All the Synoptics include statements made to Jesus while He was on the cross. When we review the statements made to Jesus, we come away with a stunning fact. Most of those who spoke to Him shouted some variation of the theme, "Save yourself." They were taunting Him with the insinuation that since He considered Himself a Savior, He should prove it by saving Himself. They reasoned that He was alive to make sinners alive so why shouldn't He come down from the cross and establish His claim. The critics did not understand Jesus had not come to save Himself; He came to save others!

The unusual interchange between the criminals around Jesus is unique to Luke's Gospel. According to the other Synoptics the two criminals on the right and left of Jesus joined in criticizing and mocking Him. At first they both insulted Jesus and suggested He should not only save Himself but, while He was at it, He could save them too. Obviously they didn't expect that to happen and were merely joining the chorus of detractors gathered around the cross (Matt. 27:44; Mark 15:32).

Only Luke reveals one of the criminals had a change of heart. While the first "railed" at Jesus, the second "rebuked" the first in spite of the fact he had originally joined in the mockery. The second man's comments inform the reader about the indisputable guilt of the other two men crucified that day. The repentant criminal admitted the guilt of both. Did they know each other? Perhaps they had joined in on some crime and had been condemned together for the same offense. In some way he knew the other man was as guilty as he was and deserved the punishment of crucifixion. By that he must have meant they were aware of the punishment if they were caught.

The second criminal's thoughts had turned away from ridiculing Jesus and trying to shift blame elsewhere. He now admitted his own guilt, and his thoughts turned to the judgment to come. He asked the first criminal, "Do you not fear God?" (23:40). In addition to accepting his own guilt, Luke is careful to use the condemned man's testimony to drive home from one more unlikely and unexpected source what must be understood about Jesus's crucifixion: Jesus was innocent.

Luke demonstrated from multiple sources the innocence of Jesus. The Roman governor Pilate found no reason to crucify Jesus. The churlish tetrarch Herod Antipas found nothing in Jesus worthy of death. Now a guilty, condemned criminal declares, "This man has done nothing wrong" (v. 41).

The criminal knew Jesus was more than a religious teacher. He recognized Jesus as a King. In his final words the thief pleaded, "Jesus, remember me when you come into your kingdom" (v. 42). Had he heard Jesus preach in some previous setting? Were Jesus's words about forgiving His killers enough to sway the criminal's opinion? Whatever stimulated the criminal's change of heart, he got good news that day. Jesus turned to him and reassured the guilty man that his simple, last-minute faith was enough. Jesus said, "Truly, I say to you, today you will be with me in paradise" (v. 43).

If there is a passage of Scripture that encourages us never to lose hope, it must be the story of the thief on the cross. Jesus demonstrated once again He had come for a single purpose: to seek and to save the lost.

"Father, into Your Hands" (vv. 44-47)

Six hours had passed since Jesus had been nailed to the cross. He was nearing His final moments. An unusual, deep darkness crowded out the sun's light from the sky. In the temple the massive curtain that hung between the holy place and the holy of holies was suddenly torn in two. Symbolically all that had stood between God and man was now erased. The torn curtain was a sign that we now have access into God's presence as never before. The scene as portrayed by Luke could hardly be more dramatic.

On the cross Jesus prayed again. His first words had been a prayer beginning with the endearing term "Father" (v. 34). Now, hours later, His confidence in His relationship with God was undiminished by the searing pain. He cried out for the last time, "Father" (v. 46). This time Jesus's prayer was not an intercession for others but a surrender of Himself. "Into your hands I commit my spirit!" With those final words the greatest human being who ever lived died.

Luke chooses that griping, emotional moment to drive home one of his consistent themes. A Roman centurion overseeing the crucifixion, presumably as he had done countless other times in his role as a military leader, declared Jesus to be an "innocent" man (v. 47).

In the three final statements of Jesus, Luke presents us with a sympathetic Savior who loves and longs to forgive sinners. His last words are enough to encourage your first steps toward Him for forgiveness and salvation.

For Memory and Meditation

"And Jesus said, 'Father, forgive them, for they know not what they do.'" (Luke 23:34)

[1]Jason A. Whitlark and Mikeal C. Parsons, "The 'Seven' Last Words: A Numerical Motivation for the Insertion of Luke 23.24a," *New Testament Studies* 52, no. 2 (April 2006): 188–204, https://doi.org/10.1017/S0028688506000117.

[2]Joel B. Green, *The Gospel of Luke*, The New International Commentary on the New Testament (Grand Rapids, MI: Wm. B. Eerdmans, 1997), 818.

Chapter 11

The First Easter Sermon

Luke 24:13-35

I was excited to preach my first Easter sermon. During my senior year in college, I was the pastor of a rural church of about forty-five loving people. The church leaders told me on Easter Sunday we might see all fifteen pews in the small church nearly filled!

I can't remember exactly what I preached, but I know in those early days I was on fire to examine and prove every detail of the Easter story. I wanted everyone to know everything about Jesus and His resurrection.

Ironically, in one of His first appearances after the resurrection on that first Easter Sunday, Jesus preached too, to a tiny congregation of two men. Jesus didn't even seem to mind when His disciples failed to recognize Him at first. Instead, His focus was on the comprehensive message He preached that day. It was like none they had ever heard.

After Jesus left them, the men who saw Him and heard that message felt like a fire had been lit in their souls. Today, the first Easter sermon of Jesus still lights fires in the hearts of believers all over the world.

The Empty Tomb (vv. 1-12)

Luke wastes no time confirming the resurrection of Jesus. Several women, who were followers of Jesus, had gone to the tomb early on that Sunday morning and discovered it was open and the body of Jesus was missing. As the women were looking inside the tomb and processing the unexpected turn of events, two men "in dazzling apparel" (v. 4), previously unseen, appeared to confirm the resurrection of Jesus. The women were terrified by the unusual duo, but the message was unmistakably clear: "Why do you seek the living among the dead? He is not here, but has risen. Remember how he told you, while he was still in Galilee, that the Son of Man must be delivered into the hands of sinful men and be crucified and on the third day rise" (vv. 5-7). The women remembered the promise of Jesus but probably couldn't yet understand all of the implications of the good news. They were the first to learn that Jesus, who had been dead, was alive again!

The women hurried back to inform the apostles of the empty tomb and the unusually dressed strangers (the Greek word describing their "dazzling" robes is used only one other time by Luke to describe a flash of lightning and is the word from which we derive the English word *star*). There was immediate skepticism among the group (v. 11).

Initial examples of doubt about the resurrection among the disciples are confirmed by all of the Gospels (Matt. 28:17; Mark 16:11; John 20:25). The doubt actually helps demonstrate how true the story of Jesus is. If the entire event had been concocted by the church, it is unlikely they would have portrayed the main protagonists of the story as doubters, skeptics, and unbelievers when news of the resurrection first came to them. Also, if the resurrection was a hoax, why would first-century men use women as the first eyewitnesses since, in that day, women were usually not regarded as credible witnesses in court?[1] So if Luke fabricated this event, we are left with two unlikely scenarios. First, Luke (and the other Gospel writers) used women with little credibility as the first witnesses, which in Roman culture would have weakened the viability of their "ruse." Second, the men who would emerge as leaders of the movement and the outspoken messengers of the resurrection didn't initially believe it themselves. Both of these odd developments point to a true event with all of the unpredictability of reality rather than a well-crafted, manufactured tale.

In spite of his initial doubts, Peter immediately ran to the tomb to see for himself and found the linen clothes that had previously wrapped the body. He left the tomb "marveling" (v. 12), a word that suggests he was leaning toward belief in the resurrection but also suggests he wasn't sure yet what to think. Obviously, he would need, and receive, more information shortly, but the empty tomb was a powerful witness to a miracle.

Confusion on the Road to Emmaus (vv. 13-24)

As is common in Luke, Jesus's actions often center around events that did not involve the well-known apostles. After Peter went into the tomb, Luke completely shifts away from the apostles and the activities in Jerusalem. What follows is an event recorded only by Luke that persuasively incorporates some of the consistently expected Lukan themes.

Somewhere near Jerusalem was a town called Emmaus, mentioned only one time in the New Testament.

Two previously unknown disciples of Jesus were walking from Jerusalem to Emmaus on the Sunday of the resurrection. They had already heard about the empty tomb and the testimony of the women and were wondering what it all meant. From their perspective the news had traveled through Jerusalem like wildfire since they concluded everyone in the city was talking about nothing else (v. 18). As they were walking and talking, Jesus Himself walked up beside them. As in other instances, He was not immediately recognizable to them (see John 20:11-16). Luke suggests their lack of recognizing the Lord was God's work since "their eyes were kept from recognizing him" (Luke 24:16).

With the advantage of anonymity, Jesus asked them to tell Him what they were so obviously concerned about. After expressing their astonishment that He didn't already know about the trending conversation of the day, one of them, Cleopas, explained to Him about "Jesus of Nazareth" (v. 19). Cleopas regarded Jesus as a mighty prophet of God and perhaps more. He outlined to the stranger the details concerning the crucifixion and laid the blame for the cross at the feet of the chief priests. Every reader must remember, as they read the Gospels, the writers have their own reasons for including the information they did. Luke expertly hits the same themes repeatedly to make his case on a range of subjects, including the accountability of the priests and religious leaders in the death of Jesus.

Cleopas expressed his disappointment about the cross, since he and others had hoped Jesus was to be a redeemer for Israel (v. 21). He continued the story by including the detail about the women going early to the tomb that morning. From Cleopas we learn conclusively that the two men in dazzling robes were regarded as "angels" (v. 23). He also suggested more leaders other than Peter, from among the disciples, had visited the empty tomb and all had corroborated at least that part of the women's testimony (v. 24).

The tone of Cleopas's telling of the story has a defeated ring to it and indicates he was still a late adopter concerning the resurrection. Like many people Cleopas probably wanted to believe but wanted more evidence. He was about to get it!

Jesus Preaches the Easter Sermon (vv. 25-29)

Jesus had spent most of His ministry preaching and teaching to crowds so large they sometimes threatened to become unmanageable or unsustainable due to their size (5:1; 9:10-17). Large crowds always seem to lend credibility to political causes, successful entertainers in concerts, and sporting events requiring high-priced tickets. The large crowds Jesus attracted excited the average people but actually helped fuel the fears and suspicions of His opponents and, ultimately, their desire to kill Him since they panicked and thought the whole world had started to follow Him (John 12:19).

So it is more than a little interesting that when Jesus comes to preach His first sermon after the resurrection, He chooses to preach to a congregation of two. One is a man we have never heard of before and will never hear of again. The other is his unnamed, anonymous, traveling companion. They are on the road to a town we've never heard of, and they are in conversation with a Savior they don't recognize! And in spite of the fact all His closest disciples are in Jerusalem wondering what has happened, Jesus stays with the two unknown disciples on the way to Emmaus all day. The entire event is nothing short of amazing.

In this unique story, found nowhere else but in the Gospel of Luke, we are reminded again of Luke's consistent theme: God's love for forgotten and marginalized people. Luke loves to tell stories that defy conventional wisdom or run contrary to the normal formulas for success.

In Luke, Samaritans are heroes when priests refuse to help. Women are evangelists when apostles fail to believe. The Messiah is born in a stable, in a small town, to poor parents. Finally, the Savior is executed as a criminal and is reviled by everyone from the religious leaders to a guilty criminal also hanging and dying on a cross. Luke now comes to the resurrection, and the Messiah who defeated death preaches to a congregation of two.

Regardless of a person's liabilities or setbacks in life, Luke presents us with a Savior who is for the disregarded and the undervalued. Jesus shuns the spectacle of declaring His resurrection in the temple courts and goes out of town to intercept two unknown disciples instead. Jesus is the people's Savior. He is anointed to preach good news to the poor, the prisoner, the blind, and the oppressed, even if it means coming back from the dead to preach that good news in the middle of nowhere to a couple of unknown, regular guys on their way home from the Passover celebration.

Jesus started His Easter sermon by reminding the two disciples that the cross was not a tragedy or a hopeless end to their dreams of redemption. Instead, the crucifixion was the plan of God, predicted hundreds of years earlier by the Jewish prophets of the Old Testament. In other words, Jesus wasn't a casualty in the battle between the religious leaders and Himself. The cross wasn't an example of Jesus's going to Jerusalem and being ground up as the first victim in His doomed revolution. The cross was victory! It was the fulfillment of Old Testament prophecies that "the Christ should suffer these things and enter into his glory" (Luke 24:26).

Have you ever played the game where you answer a question about a point of history you would like to be a part of, if you could go back? A few years ago during a staff retreat when we had welcomed several new staff members onto our team, we wanted an icebreaker to help get to know one another beyond merely our resumes. So we asked the question, "If you could go back to any time or place in history for one day, where and when would it be?" We let each person pick two or three times and places to make it interesting. I would choose the day of Pentecost and the walk to Emmaus. Why? The sermon Jesus preached on that resurrection Sunday must have been the most informative message ever preached! "And beginning with Moses and all the Prophets, he interpreted to them in all the Scriptures the things concerning himself" (v. 27).

Can you imagine that message? Jesus Himself preaching an exposition of the entire Old Testament where He is predicted or discussed has got to stand as the greatest sermon ever preached. Unfortunately, Luke only mentions it; he doesn't allow us to listen in. Fortunately, Jesus's disciples would write down several letters and reflections based on this message, and we do have that compilation. It's the New Testament!

The resurrection is good news for sinners, but it also vindicated the many prophets who spent their lives anticipating a Messiah and died having only seen Him by faith. More than that, the resurrection reveals Jesus as the one the entire Old Testament points us to. It also shows why the Old Testament is still considered Scripture by New Testament believers. It's our Bible too!

The fact that Jesus is the fulfillment of the Old Testament develops as a major theme for Luke in the resurrection accounts (vv. 44-47). Christ suffered for a reason, and resurrection was always part of the plan.

Recognition and Combustion (vv. 28-35)

It has become common to see the moments captured on news clips or social media when American military service members come home secretly to surprise their families for holidays or special life events. Usually there is a brief, split-second pause when the child or spouse doesn't recognize or realize the person in front of them is their dad or their husband. Then the moment of recognition is a powerful explosion of love and emotion as the family members race to embrace their loved one. It gets me every time.

As Jesus completed His incredible overview of the Old Testament, the two disciples were still unaware of who He was, but they must have been amazed at what they had just heard. They invited Jesus into one of their homes for food and lodging as a way of showing respect and perhaps to ask questions and learn more from this unusual and knowledgeable Bible teacher. As they ate the meal, the moment of recognition occurred. "When he was at table with them, he took the bread and blessed and broke it and gave it to them. And their eyes were opened, and they recognized him. And he vanished from their sight" (vv. 30-31). As Jesus broke the bread, they recognized Him. At that instant He was gone. Some have suggested they saw the nail marks in His hands as he broke the bread. Perhaps. The text does not say, and it is speculative. But it is a miraculous event that built the faith of two men who had started the day discouraged and ended the day as part of a history-making miracle.

The two men started talking simultaneously with understandable excitement. They agreed the words of Jesus, as He taught the Scripture, ignited a fire inside their hearts. "They said to each other, 'Did not our hearts burn within us while he talked to us on the road, while he opened to us the Scriptures?'" (v. 32).

Luke is making a subtle but important point here that will have a lasting impact on the witness of the church. The two disciples are obviously excited Jesus appeared to them because they now know He is alive! So nothing should be suggested that would diminish the understandable joy that Jesus defeated death. Still, something else is obviously happening under the surface of the narrative. The thing that set their hearts ablaze was not recognizing Jesus. Their hearts were on fire before they knew it was Him. The real volcano erupting in their souls started boiling when the Word was explained to them.

This is an understated but significantly critical point. By the time Luke had written this Gospel, the early church had already experienced explosive growth, but few people had actually seen the resurrected Jesus. The continued worldwide growth and health of the church would depend on something other than eyewitness experiences with Jesus. Instead, Luke makes clear the Word of God, when explained as a revelation about Jesus from start to finish, would be the tool the Holy Spirit would powerfully use to transform people's lives. As a result, when we read or hear or teach the Word of God, it sets our hearts on fire.

One day I was witnessing in a benevolence ministry where food, clothing, and baby supplies were distributed by a church. I started conversations with everyone who came in. My objective was to share the gospel with everyone I could and give them a New Testament. One day I spoke to a young woman while she was looking through baby clothes. She looked like she might have been in her late teens or early twenties. She had a warm disposition and a friendly way about her, but her eyes looked anxious.

As soon as I said hello and introduced myself as a minister, she informed me in Spanish she did not speak English. That wasn't unusual in the neighborhood where I was working since about 60 percent of the people spoke English as a second language or not at all. Fortunately the ministry had several Spanish New Testaments on hand.

With my limited Spanish I led her to read previously marked passages that outline the way to be saved. She gladly read each verse, and when she finished, I asked if she understood. When she said yes, I moved on to the next passage. When we reached Romans 10:13, something happened that I will never forget. In her own language, with no explanation from me, as she read, "Everyone who calls on the name of the Lord will be saved," she burst into tears.

Her tears didn't just roll from her eyes; they shot out and slashed against the page she was reading.

That day, using the guide in the back of the New Testament, I was able to lead that young lady to Christ. What had actually happened? It was not an example of my evangelistic persuasion since I could not speak her language. The Word of God changed her life. The Bible has power in itself.

For the last two thousand years billions of people have become disciples of Jesus, even though they never saw Him in the flesh, because they were exposed to the same message of the cross and resurrection the disciples heard on the way to Emmaus. The Scripture lights a fire in our souls, whether we are hearing it for the first time or studying it daily for a lifetime. When we are exposed to God's Word in power, our "hearts burn within us"!

For Memory and Meditation

"They said to each other, 'Did not our hearts burn within us while he talked to us on the road, while he opened to us the Scriptures?'" (Luke 24:32)

---

[1]Joel B. Green, *The Gospel of Luke*, The New International Commentary on the New Testament (Grand Rapids, MI: Wm. B. Eerdmans, 1997), 840.

Chapter 12

The Promise of Power

Luke 24:44-49

The world is running out of oil. At least that's the conclusion of one of the largest oil companies in the world. Their projections suggest the world has a little more than fifty years of oil left. If true, barring drastic changes, the world's major energy source is running out of gas![1]

Of course, other energy options are available, such as greater use of wind, solar, nuclear, and electric power; but regardless where we get it, access to energy will always be a top priority for our world's growing population. We all need power from somewhere.

The same is true in our spiritual lives. We need power to do what God has called us to do. The church in the United States continues to find itself in a growing secular and sometimes hostile culture. A serious look at the church in America suggests at least two things. The first is this: we are not making the impact on culture we want to make. The second observation has to do with our ability to change the direction in which we are headed now. Do we have the ability to change course? No matter how doctrinally sound we are or how many well-planned strategies our insightful leaders develop, we will never make a spiritual difference without spiritual power.

The good news is we do not have an energy shortage in the kingdom of God! The power available to the early church, which worked powerfully in the believers who turned their "world upside down" (Acts 17:6), is available to us. But if we do not avail ourselves of that power, we will not see the results seen by the early church.

The Unfinished Task (vv. 46-48)

After the resurrection of Jesus Christ, He appeared to a handful of His disciples, and He gave them a responsibility. Jesus assigned them the challenging mission of taking His message to the entire world. The question they must have been asking themselves was, "How do we do it?"

They had no money. They had no political clout. They had no particular strategy. Instead, they had a mostly undeveloped organization made up of a few men who had spent their entire lives, until the previous three years, around the Sea of Galilee.

They only had access to the transportation and communication tools of an ancient world. Most of them had likely never been out of the country of Israel and probably had a limited, provincial, and mostly negative perspective about life in the great cities of the Roman Empire.

Would the new mission require personal sacrifice? Would it require an unusual sense of devotion? The answer to those questions is an unqualified yes, and these men seemed unwilling at times to rise to the occasion. They were sometimes guilty of internal rivalries. They occasionally vacillated and showed moments of cowardice. They even fell asleep when the Lord invited them to pray for Him. Their level of personal willingness, determination, and passion would not be enough to take them around the world with the gospel, and they knew it.

Following Jesus's mandate to go internationally with the message was going to require something more than they had. Their mission, as well as ours, requires something from heaven. They needed the Holy Spirit's power. Nothing has changed. We need the power of God's Holy Spirit to energize the church today if we hope to take the gospel to our lost family, friends, cities, and the nations of the world.

Jesus, the Bible Teacher (vv. 44-48)

Jesus spent at least three years in the constant presence of a dozen men, modeling His mission. Eleven of those men were still with Him after He rose from the dead. In the days between His resurrection and ascension, He spent even more time with those eleven to prepare them to continue His ministry.

The timeline of events in Luke's Gospel is compressed. As is often the case in Scripture, details that do not serve the purposes of the author are left out of the text. Often, therefore, events seem to be occurring at the same time, when in reality they are separated by days, weeks, or longer and the time difference is simply not mentioned. In the case of Luke's description of the time between the resurrection and ascension, it seems as if little time had passed when, in fact, Jesus appeared to His disciples over a period of forty days.

In the conclusion of his Gospel, Luke merely gives us a high-level summary, an overview of events, rather than a minute-by-minute description of all the related details surrounding the last events of Jesus's time on earth. In Luke's sequel, the book of Acts, he gives us more detail about those days. It is, therefore, actually Luke himself who supplies us with the additional information about the forty days (Acts 1:3).

Near the end of those days, Jesus brought His followers together to explain what they should teach, how big their task would be, how to prepare for it, and what would ultimately be required to get it done.

Jesus told the apostles the same thing He had said to the disciples on the road to Emmaus: namely, He is the central theme of the entire Old Testament. He said, "These are my words that I spoke to you while I was still with you, that everything written about me in the Law of Moses and the Prophets and the Psalms must be fulfilled" (Luke 24:44).

Jesus used a common description of the Old Testament when He referred to the Law of Moses, the Prophets, and the Psalms. All thirty-nine books of our Old Testament are included in those categories.

Jesus's statement about the message of the Old Testament forces us to decide what we believe about Jesus. Who else, for instance, could have the temerity to assemble a group of grown men, some with families, and tell them to abandon all they had ever known and go all over the world telling everyone about Him?

Furthermore, who would claim that they are the central message of the Hebrew Scriptures? Whoever would dare to claim such a thing would either have mental health issues or would be the biggest con man and fraud in history, or He would be God. Since Jesus had died a terrible death on the cross and was raised to life a few days later, claiming to have all power and authority in heaven and on earth (Matt. 28:18), the apostles knew Jesus was the promised Messiah.

So Jesus had good reason to teach His apostles what the Old Testament said about Him. As we mentioned in the previous chapter, we needn't worry that we never received a written version of Jesus's explanation of the Old Testament. In fact, we do have it. It is our New Testament. How do we know? For one thing, much of our New Testament was written by the men who heard the teaching Luke refers to in verse 44. In that group of eleven men were Matthew, who wrote the popular Gospel bearing his name, and John, who wrote a large Gospel bearing his name, the book of Revelation, and three other smaller books. Peter was there, too, and he wrote two books bearing his name and is widely regarded as the source behind Mark's Gospel. Jesus's half brothers James and Jude became followers of Jesus soon after He was raised from the dead. They each wrote a book in the New Testament. Those five authors were responsible for eleven of the twenty-seven New Testament books, including three of the Gospels (when we allow for Peter's direct influence on Mark).

Of course Paul was not there originally, but the apostle Peter verifies Paul's writings are "Scripture" (2 Pet. 3:15-16). Paul wrote thirteen New Testament letters bearing his name after he had received a direct commission and vision from the ascended Christ. Paul's frequent traveling companion and co-minister, Luke (who was discipled by Paul), wrote the two longest books of our New Testament after carefully studying the history, talking with numerous eyewitnesses, and accumulating and using every additional written source he could find. That leaves only the book of Hebrews. No one is certain who wrote it, though few would dispute the similarities of theology common among some of Paul's close circle of co-laborers.

Therefore, this small, close-knit group of nine authors—all either apostles or close apostolic associates—wrote our New Testament. They retained for us and provided to us both the message of Jesus, as revealed in the entire Old Testament, and the teachings and actions of Jesus during His life and ministry.

In addition to the fact the authors of the New Testament were either personally discipled by Jesus or influenced by those who were, Jesus had promised the Holy Spirit would lead them to remember what He had taught them during their three years together. On the night before He went to the cross, Jesus said, "But the Helper, the Holy Spirit, whom the Father will send in my name, he will teach you all things and bring to your remembrance all that I have said to you" (John 14:26). Many years later Peter testified to the truth of that promise when he wrote:

> For we did not follow cleverly devised myths when we made known to you the power and coming of our Lord Jesus Christ, but we were eyewitnesses of his majesty. For when he received honor and glory from God the Father, and the voice was borne to him by the Majestic Glory, "This is my beloved Son, with whom I am well pleased," we ourselves heard this very voice borne from heaven, for we were with him on the holy mountain. And we have the

prophetic word more fully confirmed, to which you will do well to pay attention as to a lamp shining in a dark place, until the day dawns and the morning star rises in your hearts, knowing this first of all, that no prophecy of Scripture comes from someone's own interpretation. For no prophecy was ever produced by the will of man, but men spoke from God as they were carried along by the Holy Spirit. (2 Pet. 1:16-21)

Peter was an eyewitness, but he said the New Testament Scripture had been written through the apostles by the power of the Holy Spirit, not merely from their own recollections or impressions. This is exactly what Jesus had promised.

In light of all of this, we can be certain we have the same information available about Jesus to teach and preach in our world today. But knowing what to teach does not guarantee our teaching will be with the persuasive power of the early church. For that we will need the same anointing they had from the Holy Spirit.

The Main Thing (vv. 45-48)

Jesus must have known the apostles were experiencing information overload, so He "opened their minds to understand the Scriptures" (v. 45). In other words, Jesus gave them spiritual illumination to understand the Word of God and get to the heart of the message. Today the Holy Spirit does the same thing for us when we ask Him for help as we study or teach the Word.

Jesus instructed His apostles to proclaim a focused

message. He interpreted the biblical message to be His cross, resurrection, and the necessity of proclaiming repentance and forgiveness throughout the world. He said, "Thus it is written, that the Christ should suffer and on the third day rise from the dead, and that repentance for the forgiveness of sins should be proclaimed in his name to all nations, beginning from Jerusalem" (vv. 46-47). Jesus said His followers would be "witnesses of these things" (v. 48).

The word *witness* implies more than merely being an observer as the original disciples had been. The Greek word for "witness" is *marturio* from which we derive our English word *martyr*. It originally came from the language of the courtroom and meant "a witness" in the same sense we use it today in the legal system. Witnesses are responsible for telling what they know. Knowing about the information isn't enough. We eventually have to speak up and tell what we know. That's what Jesus meant when He said the earliest disciples as well as the most recent disciples are called upon to proclaim His message of the cross and resurrection as witnesses.

The Need for Power (v. 49)

What we need, in order to finish the work, is not merely organizational or denominational strategies. The only thing that's going to work today is supernatural. We need to see the power of God, the Holy Spirit of God, upon our churches and our ministries as never before. Otherwise we can expect more of what we have and less of what we really want.

Consider the original apostles. If ever there was a group

ready to go on a mission trip, we would think the apostles were ready. They had been Jesus's constant, handpicked traveling companions for about three years. They had seen every miracle and heard every sermon. They had prayed with Him and had been personally corrected and trained by Him.

They were eyewitnesses of the resurrection of Jesus and had studied under His private tutelage for weeks after His conquest over death. Who could be more ready to go tell the world about Jesus? But surprisingly, Jesus said they weren't ready yet! Without the power of the Holy Spirit, they were not appropriately equipped for the task of Christian ministry. If they weren't ready without the Spirit, what does that say about our readiness to witness, teach, and minister in Jesus's name if we're not Spirit filled?

Jesus said, "And behold, I am sending the promise of my Father upon you. But stay in the city until you are clothed with power from on high" (v. 49). Those words should resonate throughout every church in our country! Regardless of our denomination or ethnicity or anything else, we are helpless without the Holy Spirit.

The Promise

The Holy Spirit is not merely an option in the Christian life for some believers; He is the One promised by the Father to further the mission of Jesus throughout the earth until He returns. In other words, spiritual empowerment is God's will for His church for all time. If we are not open to the Spirit's ministry, we are resisting God's plan for our church and our personal life.

Jesus told the disciples He would take personal responsibility in sending the Spirit to fulfill His Father's will. No believer is living the Christian life Jesus wants for us if we do not recognize and welcome the collaborative effort of the Trinity to equip us for service.

Don't Move!

Jesus told the disciples (who were probably itching to get started) to "stay in the city." The Greek word translated "stay" literally means "don't move." I wonder if we fail to live Spirit-filled lives because we are prone to activism? I have seen Christians operate by a philosophy of "ready, fire, aim," and completely disregard the need for waiting for the power of God. This overly confident attitude about what we're capable of without the Spirit may be the single greatest reason we are as spiritually impotent in a lost world as we frequently are. God never promised to bless our flesh or our strength. He wants a church filled with His power, rather than a church impressed with its own efforts and ideas apart from Him.

How did the early church interpret the command to "stay in the city"? Luke tells us. They launched an unceasing prayer meeting! They spent part of their time worshipping God in the temple (v. 53) and the rest of their time praying around the clock in the upper room of a home somewhere near the temple in Jerusalem (Acts 1:14).

Their commitment to prayer is an indictment on the modern church unless we are committed to becoming houses of prayer. We won't have what they had if we won't do what they did. If we are to experience the power of the Holy Spirit as He is observed in the New Testament, we must pray as never before, join with other believers in frequent prayer meetings, and operate our churches as places distinguished by our relentless commitment to prayer.

Prayer is also a major theme of Luke's Gospel. Luke mentions prayer twenty-one times in his Gospel and twenty-five times in Acts. This is a far more frequent mention of prayer than we find in the other Synoptic Gospels.[2]

We see from the example of the early church that we "stay in the city" (metaphorically speaking) when we are aggressively committed to prayer. When we wait in prayer, we are positioning our churches to accomplish more for the Kingdom than we have ever accomplished by constant human effort.

Clothed with Power

Jesus described the Spirit-filled life with a word picture. He said the Spirit will come upon a praying church or believer in the way a person puts on a suit of clothes. Think about it. Would you leave your house for work without clothing? It's a ludicrous thought, but without the Spirit the church is naked and unprepared for ministry in the world. But we shouldn't think of being clothed in the Spirit as putting on what we once called our "Sunday clothes." The Greek word translated "clothed" is *enduo*, from which we get our English word *endowed*. The Spirit clothes us with "work clothes"! He endows us with the equipment we need to get the job done.

Jesus said the praying church would be endowed with power. The Greek word translated "power" is *dunamai*, from which we get our words *dynamic*, *dynamo*, and *dynamite*! The Greek word basically refers to the ability to accomplish a task. In other words, if Jesus sends us into the world to witness, the Holy Spirit makes it possible for us to do it effectively.

The early church experienced the "power from on high" after they had prayed for ten days. The Holy Spirit descended upon the praying church just before 9:00 a.m. on the Jewish Festival of Pentecost in Jerusalem, fifty days after Jesus's resurrection. The Spirit was the power from heaven (Acts 2:1-4).

From the time of the resurrection until Pentecost, not one person is recorded as having been converted to Christ. When the church was filled with the Holy Spirit, however, three thousand people from an international crowd representing the global reach of the gospel repented, believed the gospel, were baptized, and joined the apostle's daily Bible study after only one sermon (Acts 2:1-42)! The church was born in that moment.

Now What?

Luke gives us a treasure of information about Jesus and the Christian life we find nowhere else. He started his Gospel by describing a Spirit-filled priest in Jerusalem, his Spirit-filled wife Elizabeth, and their Spirit-filled son John the Baptist. He introduced us to a virgin in Nazareth overshadowed by the power of the Holy Spirit. Virtually everything in Luke's Gospel is saturated in the Holy Spirit's presence and ministry. So it should come as no surprise that Luke concludes his Gospel with an unfulfilled promise about the Spirit. It is an unfulfilled promise only in this sense: Luke does not mention the coming of the Spirit, in answer to their prayer, in his Gospel. What we are left with in Luke is an invitation to the church to be filled with the Spirit. In Luke's next volume the early church would pray, seek, and receive the power of the Spirit. Then they experienced the fulfillment of the promise and power.

We have reached the end of Luke's unparalleled Gospel, and he leaves us with a literary cliff-hanger. The power of the Holy Spirit is available. Will the church pray and seek the Spirit's power? Will you? If you do, you'll live an unparalleled life!

For Memory and Meditation

"You are witnesses of these things. And behold, I am sending the promise of my Father upon you. But stay in the city until you are clothed with power from on high." (Luke 24:48-49)

---

[1]Matt Dilallo, *"The World Has 53.3 Years of Oil Left,"* USA TODAY MONEY, *USA TODAY,* June 28, 2014, https://www.usatoday.com /story/money/business/2014/06/28/the-world-was-533-years-of-oil -left/11528999/

[2]Robert H. Stein, *Luke,* New American Commentary (Nashville: B&H Publishing Group, 1992), 51.

Auxano Press
Non-Disposable
Curriculum

- Designed for use in any small group
- Affordable, biblically based, and life oriented
- Choose your own material and stop and start times
- Study the Bible and build a Christian library

Auxano
PRESS

For teaching guides and additional small group study materials, or to learn about other Auxano Press titles, visit Auxanopress.com.